Editor
Eric Migliaccio

Managing Editor
Ina Massler Levin, M.A.

Illustrator
Clint McKnight

Cover Artist
Brenda DiAntonis

Art Production Manager
Kevin Barnes

Art Coordinator
Renée Christine Yates

Imaging
Craig Gunnell

Publisher

Mary D. Smith, M.S. Ed.

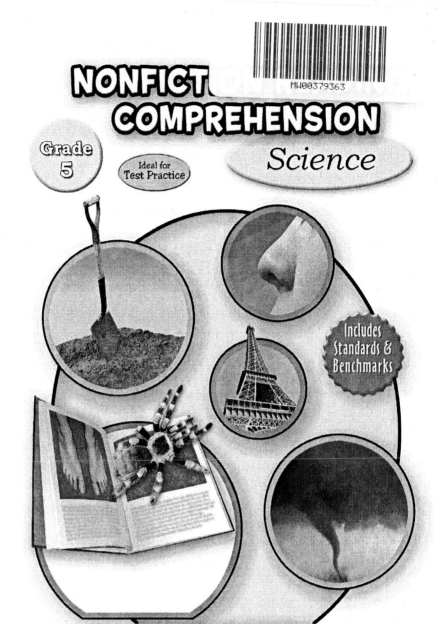

NONFICTION COMPREHENSION
Science

Grade 5

Ideal for Test Practice

Includes Standards & Benchmarks

Author

Ruth Foster, M.Ed.

Teacher Created Resources, Inc.
6421 Industry Way
Westminster, CA 92683
www.teachercreated.com
ISBN: 978-1-4206-8028-7
© 2007 Teacher Created Resources, Inc.
Reprinted, 2012
Made in U.S.A.

Teacher Created Resources

Table of Contents

Introduction

* **Science is thrilling.**

  Think of how termites eat their own skin to survive.

* **It has changed our world.**

  Think of the number of people alive today because of organ transplants.

* **It affects our lives daily.**

  Think of how aircraft are safer because cockpit windows are coated with gold.

Reading comprehension can be practiced and improved while coupled with science instruction. This book presents short, fascinating science stories. The stories were chosen to arouse curiosity; augment basic science facts and concepts taught at the fifth-grade level; and introduce a world of ideas, people, and animals.

A page of questions follows each story. These questions will provide students familiarity with different types of test questions. In addition, the practice they provide will help students develop good testing skills. Questions are written so that they lead students to focus on what was read. They provide practice for finding the main idea, as well as specific details. They provide practice in deciphering new and unknown vocabulary words. In addition, the questions encourage students to think beyond the facts. For example, every question set has an analogy question where students are expected to think about the relationship between two things and find a pair of words with the same type of relationship. Other questions provide an opportunity for students to extrapolate and consider possible consequences relevant to the information provided in the story.

The book is designed so that writing can be incorporated into every lesson. The level of writing will depend on what the teacher desires, as well as the needs of the students.

Lessons in *Nonfiction Reading Comprehension: Science, Grade 5* meet and are correlated to the Mid-continent Research for Education and Learning (McREL) standards. They are listed on page 8.

A place for *Nonfiction Reading Comprehension: Science, Grade 5* can be found in every classroom or home. It can be a part of daily instruction in time designated for both reading and science. It can be used for both group and individual instruction. Stories can be read with someone or on one's own. *Nonfiction Reading Comprehension: Science, Grade 5* can help students improve in multiple areas, including reading, science, critical thinking, writing, and test taking.

Using This Book

The Stories

Each story in *Nonfiction Reading Comprehension: Science, Grade 5* is a separate unit. For this reason, the stories can (but do not have to) be read in order. A teacher can choose any story that coincides with classroom activity.

Stories can be assigned to be read during science or reading periods. They can be used as classroom work or as supplemental material.

Each story is five paragraphs long. The stories range from 325–350 words in length. They are written at the fifth-grade level and have the appropriate sentence structure.

New Words

Each story includes a list of eight new words. Each of the new words is used a minimum of two times in the story. New words may sometimes have an addition of a simple word ending such as "s," "ed," or "ing." The new words are introduced in the story in the same order that they are presented in the new word list. Many of the new words are found in more than one story. Mastery of the new words may not come immediately, but practice articulating, seeing, and writing the words will build a foundation for future learning.

✳ A teacher may choose to have the students read and repeat the words together as a class.

✳ While it is true that the majority of the words are defined explicitly or in context in the stories, a teacher may choose to discuss and define the new words before the students begin reading. This will only reinforce sight-word identification and reading vocabulary.

✳ A teacher may engage the class in an activity where students use the new word in a sentence. Or, the teacher may use the word in two sentences. Only one sentence will use the word correctly. Students will be asked to identify which sentence is correct. For example, one new word is *encounter*. The teacher might say,

> *"One might encounter a tarantula on every continent but Antarctica."*

> *"The encounter tarantula was large enough to eat small birds."*

✳ A teacher may also allow students to choose one new word to add to their weekly spelling list. This provides students with an opportunity to feel part of a decision-making process, as well as gain "ownership" over new words. In addition, practice spelling sight words reinforces the idea that we can learn to recognize new words across stories because there is consistency in spelling.

✳ A teacher may choose to have students go through the story after it is read and circle each new word one or two times.

Using This Book *(cont.)*

The Writing Link

A teacher may choose to link writing exercises to the science stories presented in the book. All writing links reinforce handwriting and spelling skills. Writing links with optional sentence tasks reinforce sentence construction and punctuation.

✻ A teacher may choose to have a student pick one new word from the list of new words and write it out. (Space is provided.) This option may seem simple, but it provides students with opportunities to take control. The students are not overwhelmed by the task of the word write-outs because they are choosing the word. It also reinforces sight-word identification. If a teacher has begun to instruct students in cursive writing, the teacher can ask them to write out the word twice, once in print and once in cursive.

✻ A teacher may choose to have the students write out a complete sentence using one of the new words. The sentences can by formulated together as a class or as individual work. Depending on other classroom work, the teacher may want to remind students about capital letters and ending punctuation.

✻ A teacher may require the students to write out a sentence after the story questions have been answered. The sentence may or may not contain a new word. The sentence may have one of the following starts:

- I learned . . .
- Did you know . . .
- I thought . . .
- An interesting thing about . . .

If the teacher decides on this type of sentence formation, he or she may want to demonstrate how words from the story can be used to form sentences. For example, this is the second paragraph in the selection titled "A Tarantula and Duct Tape":

> *Tarantulas are the biggest spiders in the world. There are more than 850 different species, or kinds, of tarantulas. They are found on every continent except Antarctica. The largest kind is a species in South America. It is called the goliath bird-eater. Goliath bird-eater spiders are about 3.5 inches (9 cm) long. They can measure up to 11 inches (28 cm) across. This measurement includes their legs.*

Possible sample sentence write-outs may be . . .

> *"I learned that tarantulas are found on every continent except Antarctica."*

> *"I thought there was only one species of tarantulas, but there are more than 850 different species."*

> *"Did you know that the largest kind of tarantula is a species in South America?"*

> *"An interesting thing about tarantulas is that they are the biggest spiders in the world."*

This type of exercise reinforces spelling and sentence structure. It also teaches responsibility: students learn to go back to the story to check word spelling. It also provides elementary report-writing skills. Students are taking information in a story source and reporting it in their own sentence construction.

Using This Book *(cont.)*

The Questions

❋ The main-idea question pushes students to focus on the topic of what was read. It allows practice in discerning between answers that are too broad or too narrow.

❋ The specific-detail question requires students to retrieve or recall a particular fact mentioned in the story. Students gain practice referring back to a source. They also are pushed to think about the structure of the story. Where would this fact most likely be mentioned in the story? What paragraph would most likely contain the fact to be retrieved?

❋ The analogy question pushes students to develop reasoning skills. It pairs two words mentioned in the story and asks students to think about how the words relate to each other. Students are then asked to find an analogous pair. Students are expected to recognize and use analogies in all course readings, written work, and in listening. This particular type of question is found on many cognitive-functioning tests.

❋ The remaining two questions are a mixture of vocabulary, identifying what is true or not true, inference, or extrapolation questions. Going back and reading the word in context can always answer vocabulary questions. The inference questions are often the most difficult for many students, but they provide practice for what students will find on standardized tests. They also encourage students to think beyond the story and to think critically about how facts can be interpreted or why something works.

The Test Link

Standardized tests have become obligatory in schools throughout our nation and around the world. There are certain test-taking skills and strategies that can be developed by using this resource.

❋ Students can answer the questions on the page by filling in the circle of the correct answer, or you may choose to have your students use the answer sheet located at the back of the book (page 141). Filling in the bubble page provides students with practice responding in a standardized-test format.

❋ Questions are presented in a mixed-up order, though the main idea question is always placed in the numbers one, two, or three slots. The analogy question is always placed in the three, four, or five slots. This mixed-up order provides practice with standardized-test formats, where reading-comprehension passages often have main-idea questions, but these type of questions are not necessarily placed first.

Using This Book *(cont.)*

The Test Link *(cont.)*

❋ A teacher may want to point out to students that often a main-idea question can be used to help focus on what the story is about. A teacher may also want to point out that an analogy question can be done any time, since it is not crucial to the main focus of the story.

❋ A teacher may want to remind students to read every answer choice. Many students are afraid of not remembering information. Reinforcing this tip helps them to remember that on multiple-choice tests, one is identifying the best answer, not making up an answer.

❋ A teacher may choose to discuss the strategy of eliminating wrong answer choices to find the correct one. Teachers should instruct students that even if they can only eliminate one answer choice, their guess will have a better chance of being right. A teacher may want to go through several questions to demonstrate this strategy. For example, in the "A Tarantula and Duct Tape" selection there is the following question:

> **5.** From the story, one can tell that a tarantula
>
> ⓐ felt threatened by the patient.
>
> ⓑ tried to make a double puncture wound.
>
> ⓒ wanted to inject venom into the patient.
>
> ⓓ was a different species than the goliath bird-eater

The correct answer may be determined by comparing answer choices. Answers B and C are tied together. They are both mentioned in paragraphs three and four. It is explained that venom is injected through the double puncture wound made by a tarantula's fangs. If a tarantula tried to make a double puncture wound, it wanted to inject venom. If B is correct, so is C. Since they cannot both be correct, both are incorrect. At this point, a teacher can point out that one of the two remaining choices, either A or D, has to be correct. A teacher can instruct that this is a good time, if needed, to go back to the story and look for when the goliath bird-eater is mentioned (paragraph two and three). This particular species is mentioned only as an example. It is not mentioned in paragraph 5, where it is explained what a tarantula does if it feels threatened.

The Thrill of Science

The challenge of writing this book was to allow students access to the thrills of science while understanding that many science words or concepts are beyond the fifth-grade reading level. It is hoped that the range of stories and the ways concepts are presented reinforces basic science concepts, all while improving basic reading-comprehension skills. It is also hoped that the students' imaginations are whetted. After reading each story, students will want to question and explore the subject.

Meeting Standards

Listed below are the McREL standards for Language Arts Level 2 (Grades 3–5).

Copyright 2004 McREL

Mid-Continent Research for Education and Learning

2250 S. Parker Rd, Suite 500

Aurora, CO 80014

Telephone: 303-337-0990

www.mcrel.org/standards-benchmarks

McREL Standards are in **bold.** Benchmarks are in regular print. All lessons meet the following standards and benchmarks unless noted.

Uses stylistic and rhetorical aspects of writing.

- Uses a variety of sentence structures in writing (*All lessons where writing a complete sentence option is followed.*)
- Uses grammatical and mechanical conventions in written compositions

  Writes in cursive (*All lessons where teacher follows the option of writing a sentence using a new word or completion of beginning sentence options in cursive.*)

  Uses conventions of spelling, capitalization, and punctuation in writing compositions (*All lessons where teacher follows option of writing a sentence using a new word or completion of beginning sentence options.*)

Uses the general skills and strategies of the reading process.

- Previews text
- Establishes a purpose for reading
- Represents concrete information as explicit mental pictures
- Uses phonetic and structural analysis techniques, syntactic structure, and semantic context to decode unknown words
- Use a variety of context clues to decode unknown words
- Understands level-appropriate reading vocabulary
- Monitors own reading strategies and makes modifications as needed
- Adjusts speed of reading to suit purpose and difficulty of material
- Understands the author's purpose

Uses reading skills and strategies to understand a variety of informational texts.

- Summarizes and paraphrases information in texts
- Uses prior knowledge and experience to understand and respond to new information

A Tarantula and Duct Tape

These are new words to practice.

Say each word 10 times.

* encounter   * venom

* tarantula   * paralyzes

* species   * puncture

* subdue   * barbed

**Before or after reading the story, write one sentence
that contains at least one new word.**

_____

_____

_____

_____

A Tarantula and Duct Tape

A patient has had an encounter, or meeting, with a tarantula. What does the doctor do? The doctor brings out duct tape. Why would a doctor bring out duct tape when a patient has encountered a tarantula?

Tarantulas are the biggest spiders in the world. There are more than 850 different species, or kinds, of tarantulas. They are found on every continent except Antarctica. The largest kind is a species in South America. It is called the goliath bird-eater. Goliath bird-eater spiders are about 3.5 inches (9 cm) long. They can measure up to 11 inches (28 cm) across. This measurement includes their legs.

These enormous spiders take young birds from their nests. They also eat birds, frogs, and bats. They eat beetles, small rodents, and lizards, too. To subdue, or get control over, a victim, a tarantula pounces on it. Then, it spears it with two fangs. Venom, or a type of poison, is injected into the victim through the fangs. The venom kills or paralyzes the victim. When something is paralyzed, it cannot move.

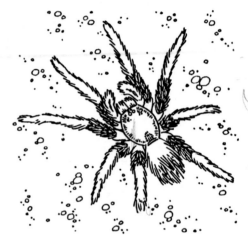

tarantula

Usually, a tarantula's venom is not strong enough to subdue a person. The person may have a painful reaction, but the person does not die. When the doctor put duct tape on the patient who had an encounter with a tarantella, the doctor checked first for a double puncture wound. A puncture is a hole made by a sharp point, such as a fang. It was only when the doctor did not see a double puncture wound and knew the patient had not been bitten that he applied the duct tape.

When a tarantula feels threatened, it can rub its back pair of legs against its abdomen. This causes thousands of tiny hairs to fly into the air. The hairs are barbed. A barb is a sharp point that is attached to an object and sticks out backward. The barbed hairs cause a painful rash—or even blindness if they land near eyes. When the doctor applied duct tape to his patient, the doctor was removing barbed hairs! The tiny hairs stuck to the sticky tape!

A Tarantula and Duct Tape

**After reading the story, answer the questions.
Fill in the circle next to the correct answer.**

1. What is *not* listed as something tarantulas eat?

   (a) ants
   (b) birds
   (c) beetles
   (d) rodents

2. This story is mainly about

   (a) the biggest tarantula species.
   (b) what duct tape can be used for.
   (c) tarantulas and why a doctor did something.
   (d) how tarantula venom is injected and what it does.

3. What is most likely to have a barb?

   (a) a pencil
   (b) a jump rope
   (c) a fishing hook
   (d) a washing machine

4. Think about how the word *subdue* relates to *control*. What two words relate in the same way?

   | subdue : control |

   (a) apply : remove
   (b) paralyze : bite
   (c) puncture : fang
   (d) encounter : meet

5. From the story, you can tell that a tarantula

   (a) felt threatened by the patient.
   (b) tried to make a double puncture wound.
   (c) wanted to inject venom into the patient.
   (d) was a different species than the goliath bird-eater.

Space Junk

These are new words to practice.
Say each word 10 times.

* debris   ~~trash~~   * exceed

* orbiting   * impact

* fragment   * abandoned

* shatter   * atmosphere

Before or after reading the story, write one sentence that contains at least one new word.

_____

_____

_____

_____

Space Junk

People are tracking junk, or debris. Debris is broken, scattered remains. It is rubbish. It is garbage. More than 10,000 pieces of debris are being tracked. All the pieces of debris have two things in common. They are all four inches (10 cm) wide or longer. They are all orbiting, or going around, Earth.

There are actually millions of fragments orbiting Earth. A fragment is a piece of something that has broken or a part that has broken away. There are too many of these fragments to track, but even small ones can do great harm. In fact, a piece as small as an apple can destroy a spacecraft. It can cause the spacecraft to shatter into hundreds of pieces.

How can a tiny piece of debris shatter a spacecraft? How can it break it into many pieces? Debris whizzes through space. Some pieces exceed, or go beyond, speeds of 17,000 miles (27,200 km) per hour! Impact is a hitting together with force. The force of impact with even a small object at great speeds is exceedingly dangerous.

The debris comes from scientific missions. It comes from manned spaceflights. It comes from the International Space Station. Space junk objects include old rocket bodies. It includes abandoned man-made satellites. When something is abandoned, it is left, or deserted. It includes bags of garbage released from the Russian space station *Mir*. It includes a glove and spatula dropped by space-shuttle astronauts. All of these junk items and many others are being tracked.

Are we safe on Earth from space debris? About once a day, some old junk enters our atmosphere. Our atmosphere is made up of the gases surrounding our planet. Several pieces of debris weighing over 100 pounds (45 kg) have crashed and hit the ground, but most space debris burns up in the atmosphere. There is only one recorded case of someone being hit by space junk. The person hit was a woman in Tulsa, Oklahoma. She was not hurt.

Mir space station

Space Junk

After reading the story, answer the questions.
Fill in the circle next to the correct answer.

1. This story is mainly about

(a) debris in space.

(b) why junk is dangerous.

(c) how fast debris can travel.

(d) objects that are being tracked.

2. In the story, space junk is not listed as coming from

(a) the atmosphere.

(b) manned spaceflights.

(c) scientific missions.

(d) the International Space Station.

3. Think about how the word *shatter* relates to *break*. What two words relate in the same way?

shatter : break

(a) crash : burn

(b) destroy : speed

(c) release : orbit

(d) abandon : desert

4. Pick the word that best completes the sentence: "This is a timed test. You must not _____ the time limit."

(a) stop

(b) exceed

(c) impact

(d) record

5. Some people think garbage from Earth should be shot into space. Why might this not be a good idea?

(a) it might burn up in the atmosphere

(b) it might travel at exceedingly fast speeds

(c) it might hit a spacecraft or fall back to Earth

(d) it might break into fragments too small to be tracked

Gorilla Lady

These are new words to practice.
Say each word 10 times.

* gorilla   * primate   monkeys apes gorillas

* foliage – leaver   * encounter   meeting

* dense   * detailed

* primatologist   * poacher

apes

Before or after reading the story, write one sentence
that contains at least one new word.

_____

_____

_____

_____

Gorilla Lady

There was a split second of warning screams and roars. Then, the gorillas, an enormous adult male and female, began their attack. Dian Fossey could feel the ground shake as the two charging beasts came close. When they were less than two feet (61 cm) away and she could clearly see their long, yellow canine teeth, Fossey dove. She dove into foliage. The foliage was a thick, dense tangle of plant and tree leaves.

The gorillas were running too fast to stop. They thundered past. Fossey said later that she was fortunate they did not return, as it took her just a second to dive into the dense foliage but at least 15 minutes to get out of it! Fossey was a primatologist. A primatologist studies primates. Primates are a group of mammals. All apes and monkeys are primates.

Dian Fossey

Through her early encounters, or meetings, with gorillas, Fossey learned how to observe gorillas safely. She would crouch low to the ground. She would not look a gorilla directly in the eye. She would let a gorilla know she was close by humming a certain way. This way the risk of startling a gorilla with a surprise encounter was greatly lessened. She would move slowly. She would let gorillas touch her, but she would never touch one first.

Fossey was the first person to do detailed studies of gorillas. By living in the wilds with them, she was able to make detailed observations. She counted them. She recorded them. She learned to recognize different family members. She observed how they behaved and what they did. She learned that they are not vicious or wicked beasts. They are shy, timid, gentle giants that eat mostly plants.

Fossey studied mountain gorillas in the Virunga Mountains. The Virunga Mountains are in Rwanda. Rwanda is a country in Africa. Unfortunately, Rwanda could not control poaching. A poacher is someone who hunts on someone else's land. Poachers were responsible for many gorilla deaths. Fossey did her best to defend the gorillas against poachers. Fossey saved many gorillas, but sadly, she was killed by poachers in 1985.

Gorilla Lady

After reading the story, answer the questions.
Fill in the circle next to the correct answer.

1. What is something Fossey learned *not* to do when she encountered gorillas?

   (a) move slowly

   (b) make a humming sound

   (c) crouch low to the ground

   (d) look a gorilla directly in the eye

2. This story is mainly about

   (a) poaching.

   (b) an attack.

   (c) a primatologist.

   (d) what gorillas eat.

3. From the story you can tell that

   (a) all primates are gentle.

   (b) all mammals are primates.

   (c) all gorillas are mammals.

   (d) all primates are gorillas.

4. Think about how the word *move* relates to *stay*. What two words relate in the same way?

move : stay

   (a) observe : look

   (b) crouch : stand

   (c) encounter : meet

   (d) startle : surprise

5. Most likely, the two gorillas charged Fossey

   (a) when a poacher was near by.

   (b) before Fossey made many gorilla observations.

   (c) because the gorillas were wicked and vicious beasts.

   (d) after Fossey learned how to safely observe gorillas.

Why We Get Goose Bumps

These are new words to practice.
Say each word 10 times.

* appear		* follicle	
* reaction		* dermis	
* conserve		* epidermis	
* scalp		* oval	

Before or after reading the story, write one sentence
that contains at least one new word.

_____

_____

_____

_____

Why We Get Goose Bumps

Tiny bumps often appear on our skin when we get cold. Many people call these bumps "goose bumps." They are also known as "goose pimples" or "cold seeds." Goose bumps are a reaction to the cold. They are the body's way of trying to conserve, or save, warmth.

When we are cold, the hairs on our body stand on end. This reaction traps a layer of warm air next to the skin. The layer of trapped air helps keep the body warm. It helps to conserve the body's heat. How does the hair stand on end? Tiny muscles pull the hair upright. The muscles cause the skin to bunch up and form a bump around each hair. Our skin appears, or seems, to be covered in "goose bumps."

The hair on top of our head does two things. It helps us to conserve heat. By trapping a layer of warm air next to our scalp, it keeps us from losing a lot of heat through our heads. It also protects our scalps from the burning rays of the sun. It prevents our scalps from getting sunburnt.

Hair on our body and on our head is made up of the shaft and the root. The root is enclosed in a tiny pit called the hair follicle. Hair follicles are embedded, or set firmly, in the part of the skin called the dermis. The dermis is the thick layer of skin that is below the epidermis. When we look at ourselves, we see a protective coat of dead skin cells covering the epidermis.

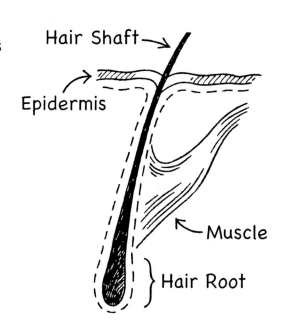

hair follicle

Although hair is made from living cells inside the hair follicles, hair is not alive. Our hair grows when new cells produced in the follicles push older cells upward. Hair follicles can be round, oval, or flat. Straight hair grows from round follicles, wavy hair grows from oval follicles, and curly hair grows from flat follicles. Whatever shape hair is, it is extremely strong. A rope made from about 1,000 strands of human hair is strong enough to lift an average adult person.

Why We Get Goose Bumps

After reading the story, answer the questions.
Fill in the circle next to the correct answer.

1. From the story, one can tell that
   ⓐ human hair makes the strongest ropes.
   ⓑ people in warm places do not need hair.
   ⓒ hair helps to protect people from the sun.
   ⓓ straight hair is stronger than curly hair.

2. This story is mainly about
   ⓐ hair.
   ⓑ skin.
   ⓒ bumps.
   ⓓ follicles.

3. It does not hurt to cut our hair because
   ⓐ our hair is not alive.
   ⓑ our hair is made from living cells.
   ⓒ our hair is pulled upright by tiny muscles.
   ⓓ our hair follicles are embedded in the dermis.

4. Think about how the word *scalp* relates to *head*. What two words relate in the same way?

   | scalp : head |

   ⓐ eye : see
   ⓑ leg : arm
   ⓒ skin : hair
   ⓓ finger : hand

5. Wavy hair grows from
   ⓐ flat follicles.
   ⓑ oval follicles.
   ⓒ round follicles.
   ⓓ square follicles.

Strange Partners

These are new words to practice.
Say each word 10 times.

* ratel   * organisms

* flutter   * symbiosis

* chirps   * larvae

* cease   * obtain

stop

Before or after reading the story, write one sentence
that contains at least one new word.

_____

_____

_____

_____

Strange Partners

A ratel, or honey badger, is peacefully resting. Suddenly, a small bird begins to flutter around the ratel's head. It chirps loudly. The bird will not leave the ratel alone. It will not cease, or stop, flapping its wings. It will not cease its determined chirping. What does the ratel do? Does the ratel attack the chirping bird fluttering around its head?

The ratel simply gets up. It does not attack the bird. Instead, it follows it. This is because the ratel and the bird are partners. Each one does something to help the other. It may seem unusual that two very different organisms, or living things, are partners. Yet strange partnerships between two uncommon organisms are found all the time in nature. Scientists call these strange types of partnership *symbiosis*. Symbiosis is when two different organisms work together.

The bird is an African honeyguide. The honeyguide eats the wormlike larvae, or young, of bees, wasps, and termites. In addition to the larvae, it eats waxy honeycomb found inside bees' nests. The honeyguide may eat bee larvae and honeycomb, but it needs help obtaining, or getting, it. This is because the bird is not strong enough to break open bees' nests.

ratel

Yet the ratel is! The ratel has long, sharp claws. It has tough, thick skin. It has thick fur. With its fur and skin to protect it from angry bees' stings, the ratel can safely and easily rip open a nest with its claws. What the ratel needs help with is finding the bees' nests. This is why the honeyguide and the ratel are a perfect team.

The keen-eyed honeyguide finds a nest, and then it looks for a ratel. The honeyguide, with its fluttering and loud chirping, guides, or leads, the ratel to the bees' nest. Once at the nest, the ratel easily rips it open. The ratel eats first, but then it is the honeyguide's turn. By teaming up, both the honeyguide and the ratel are able to obtain what they want—a feast of honey, honeycomb, and bee larvae!

Strange Partners

After reading the story, answer the questions.
Fill in the circle next to the correct answer.

1. This story is mainly about

   (a) a symbiotic team.
   (b) getting honeycomb.
   (c) unusual organisms.
   (d) a keen-eyed honeyguide.

2. Why doesn't the ratel, or honey badger, attack the honeyguide when the honeyguide will not leave it alone?

   (a) it will eat first
   (b) it is stronger than the honeyguide
   (c) it has thick fur and tough skin to protect it
   (d) it knows the honeyguide will lead it to a bee nest

3. Think about how the word *obtain* relates to *get*. What two words relate in the same way?

   | obtain : get |

   (a) cease : go
   (b) need : want
   (c) guide : lead
   (d) flutter : chirp

4. What is not an organism?

   (a) bird
   (b) larvae
   (c) termite
   (d) honeycomb

5. From the story, one can tell that ratels most likely live on the continent of

   (a) Asia.
   (b) Africa.
   (c) Europe.
   (d) North America.

A Brilliant Element

These are new words to practice.
Say each word 10 times.

* element

* visor

* atom

* film

* applied

* malleable

* brilliant

* container

Before or after reading the story, write one sentence
that contains at least one new word.

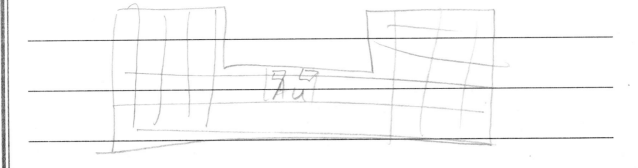

A Brilliant Element

There is an element that is put on aircraft cockpit windows. It is put on astronauts' visors. An element is a substance made up of only one type of atom. An atom is very small. An atom is the smallest amount of an element that has all the properties of that element. The element on aircraft cockpit windows and astronauts' visors is made into a very thin film, or sheet. Then, it is applied to the surface of the window and visor glass. What is the element? Why is it applied?

The element is gold. Gold is a malleable metal. When something is malleable, it is easy to shape. Something malleable can be pounded into different shapes without breaking. Like all metals, gold is a good conductor of electricity. Unlike many metals, it does not react to common substances like air and water.

Today, gold is stretched into strands thinner than a human hair. It is used in computers, phones, and other electronic gadgets. About 90 pounds (40 kg) of gold were used in the construction of the space shuttle. Gold is also used in jewelry. Thin sheets of it are used to cover buildings for decoration.

Gold's brilliant, or bright, color is because it reflects almost all of the yellow light that reaches it. The thin gold coating on the cockpit windows and visors reflects the sun's light. It helps pilots and astronauts to see and protects them from the harmful light of the sun's rays. How thick is this protective film? It is less than a millionth of an inch (2.5 cm) thick!

Every element has a symbol. The symbol for gold is Au. The symbol comes from the Latin word *aurum*. *Aurum* is the Latin word for "gold." Gold has always been a very expensive metal. One reason is that there is a limited supply. Think of a square container, or box, 55 feet high, 55 feet wide, and 55 feet long (18 m by 18 m by 18 m). All the gold in the world that has ever been mined would fit in this container.

A Brilliant Element

After reading the story, answer the questions.
Fill in the circle next to the correct answer.

1. What is the symbol for gold?

(a) Ag

(b) An

~~(c)~~ Au

(d) Aw

2. A thin film of gold is applied to aircraft cockpit windows and astronauts' visors because

(a) it is a metal.

(b) it does not react to air.

(c) it reflects the sun's light.

(d) it is a good conductor of electricity.

3. This story is mainly about

(a) atoms.

(b) an element. *gold*

(c) gold's color.

(d) how much gold there is.

4. Which statement about gold is true?

~~(a)~~ There is a limited supply.

(b) It will react to water and air.

(c) It is used in jewelry because it is a good conductor.

(d) Gold was cheap before it was used in electronic gadgets.

5. Think about how the word *malleable* relates to *shaped*. What two words relate in the same way?

malleable : shaped

(a) old : ruined

(b) big : increased

(c) yellow : colored

(d) changeable : changed

Digging a Hole to China

These are new words to practice.
Say each word 10 times.

* diameter   * core

* crust   * hypothetical

* mantle   * campus

* molten   * occasional

Before or after reading the story, write one sentence
that contains at least one new word.

_____

_____

_____

_____

Digging a Hole to China

"I am going to dig a hole to China." Many little children say this. Are you one of the many who have tried? You would have had to dig the distance of Earth's diameter to succeed. Earth's diameter measures 7,900 miles (12,640 km). This is the length of a straight line passing through the center of Earth from one side to the other.

First, you would have had to drill through Earth's crust. Earth's crust is a thin layer of rock at the Earth's surface. Second, you would have had to go through the Earth's mantle. The mantle is a layer of molten, or melted, rock. After the molten mantle, you would have to drill through the core, or center, made up of iron and nickel. Once at the center, you would have to go through the core, mantle, and crust on the other side to come out at the surface.

A hypothetical situation is not real. It is imagined. It hasn't happened. What if, hypothetically, you could dig through the Earth? Would you end up in China? If you are in North America, it is very unlikely. In fact, if you succeed, you better bring a wet suit! This is because you are most likely to come out in the middle of the ocean.

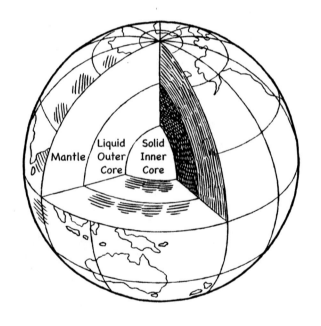

The lower 48 states are all of the states except for Alaska and Hawaii. You can dig in three places in the lower 48 and come out on land on Earth's opposite side. Two of the places you can dig are in Colorado. One place is in Montana. The places are in a town, next to a highway, and on a campus. A campus is the grounds of a college or school.

What is the land opposite these places like? Would you surprise anyone when you popped out of your hypothetical hole? At one place, you might bump into a scientist, but it would have to be a certain time of the year. At the other places, the only thing you are likely to spot is an occasional seal. When something is occasional, it happens only once in a while.

Digging a Hole to China

After reading the story, answer the questions.
Fill in the circle next to the correct answer.

1. What part of the Earth is made up of iron and nickel?

   (a) the core

   (b) the mantle

   (c) the surface

   (d) the diameter

2. This story is mainly about

   (a) where land is.

   (b) a hypothetical hole.

   (c) what is inside Earth.

   (d) how to dig a hole to China.

3. Which event below happens only occasionally?

   (a) a party

   (b) eating lunch

   (c) going to school

   (d) the change of seasons

4. Think about how the word *campus* relates to *students*. What two words relate in the same way?

   campus : students

   (a) bird : nests

   (b) corn : farms

   (c) zoo : animals

   (d) car : automobiles

5. What is the most likely reason Alaska and Hawaii are not considered part of the lower 48?

   (a) They have higher mountains.

   (b) They have different high and low temperatures.

   (c) They do not have as many people living in them.

   (d) They do not share boundaries with the other states.

A Picture to Remember

These are new words to practice.

Say each word 10 times.

* measurement   * despair

* memorize   * liquid

* mnemonic   * aid

* woe   * phrase

**Before or after reading the story, write one sentence
that contains at least one new word.**

_____

_____

_____

_____

A Picture to Remember

Ms. Franklin's unhappy students said, "We are full of woe and in despair." Ms. Franklin asked her students why they were sad and had given up hope. The students answered, "We are full of woe because of our lessons on liquid measurement. We are in despair because we are afraid we will never memorize how cups, pints, quarts, and gallons fit together. It is too hard to remember how much of one makes how much of the other!"

"I have a mnemonic aid," said Ms. Franklin. "Something that is mnemonic has to do with memory. Aid is help or assistance. A mnemonic aid helps one to remember something. Some mnemonic aids are phrases or expressions. We learned the phrase, 'Lefty loosey, righty tighty.' That mnemonic phrase helped you to remember that to open a jar or loosen most screws, you turn left. To screw on a lid or tighten most screws, you turn right."

Ms. Franklin continued, "My mnemonic aid for liquid measurement is not a phrase. It is a picture that will help you memorize how cups, pints, quarts, and gallons fit together." Ms. Franklin went to the board. First, she drew one big *G*. Then she drew four *Q*s. Two of the *Q*s were in the top half of the *G*. Two of the *Q*s were in the bottom half of the *G*. Inside each *Q*, Ms. Franklin drew two *P*s. She drew eight *P*s in total. Then she drew two *C*s in each *P*. She drew a total of sixteen *C*s.

The students looked at the picture with the sixteen *C*s, eight *P*s, four *Q*s, and one *G*. They said, "The *C* is for cup! The *P* is for pint! The *Q* is for quart! The *G* is for gallon! To know how much of one makes how much of the other, all we have to do is draw and count!

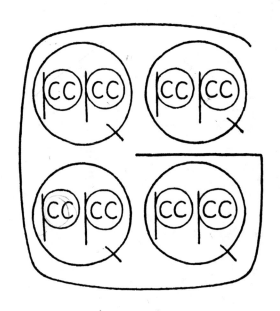

"We can see that there are two cups in a pint. We can see that there are two pints or four cups in a quart. We can see that there are sixteen cups, or eight pints, or four quarts in a gallon! We no longer feel despair! We are no longer full of woe! With this mnemonic aid, liquid measurement is easy!"

A Picture to Remember

After reading the story, answer the questions.
Fill in the circle next to the correct answer.

1. This story is mainly about

(a) Ms. Franklin.

(b) drawing pictures.

(c) being sad and full of despair.

(d) a way to remember liquid measurement.

2. One can tell from the mnemonic aid picture that

(a) there are two pints in one gallon.

(b) there are six pints in three quarts.

(c) there are eight cups in three pints.

(d) there are four quarts in two gallons.

3. Think about how the word *sad* relates to *woeful*. What two words relate in the same way?

> **sad : woeful**

(a) big : small

(b) glad : happy

(c) tired : awake

(d) brave : afraid

4. Which phrase below is a mnemonic aid?

(a) A year has 365 days.

(b) Where there is smoke, there is fire.

(c) The first letters of the Great Lakes spell HOMES.

(d) Jack and Jill went up a hill to fetch a pail of water.

5. Why might it help that most screws turn in the same direction?

(a) one will always know how many screws one needs

(b) one will always know what kind of screw to use

(c) one will always know if the screws can be big or small

(d) one will always know when one is tightening or loosening

A Whale of a Fish

These are new words to practice.
Say each word 10 times.

* plankton   * individual

* colossal   * population

* broad   * dwindling

* unique   * digital

Before or after reading the story, write one sentence
that contains at least one new word.

_____

_____

_____

_____

A Whale of a Fish

The whale shark's mouth is so big that when it is opened wide, a small car can drive into it. When the whale shark wants to eat, it just opens its wide mouth, swims forward, and sucks up plankton. Plankton is a collection of tiny animals that swim in the ocean.

The whale shark is a fish, not a whale. (Whales are mammals.) The whale shark's name came from its colossal, or huge, size. This colossal fish is the biggest fish in the world. It is bigger than many whales. Whale sharks have flat, broad (wide) heads. The whale shark's mouth is located right at the end of its flat, broad head. Its open mouth is as large as its head.

The whale shark can reach lengths of 50 feet (15 m), but the average length is 25 to 35 feet (7.5 to 8.5 m). Whale shark have a unique, or unusual, checkerboard pattern of spots on their backs. Each individual shark has a unique pattern that runs from the tip of its head to the tip of its tail. The spots are white or yellowish dots. They are separated by rows of stripes and bars, also white or yellowish.

whale shark

Scientists were worried that whale-shark populations were dwindling, or going down. They had no way of proving it. Then, scientists came up with a clever way of assigning each whale shark a "digital fingerprint." A "digital fingerprint" is based on a photograph of the pattern of spots on a whale shark's back. With a "digital fingerprint," the scientists could track individuals and population numbers.

To make "digital fingerprints" scientist used a program of the National Aeronautics and Space Administration, or NASA! How could a space program help whale sharks? NASA has a program that is used to identify stars. In the night sky, stars are a pattern of white spots on a dark background—just as a whale shark's back is a pattern of white spots on a dark background! Using NASA's program, scientists are able to track the movements of individual whale sharks. Now they can prove that the population is dwindling.

A Whale of a Fish

**After reading the story, answer the questions.
Fill in the circle next to the correct answer.**

1. This story is mainly about

   ⓐ the biggest fish.

   ⓑ digital fingerprints.

   ⓒ the mouth of a whale shark.

   ⓓ how NASA helped track whale sharks.

2. Why would scientists want a "digital fingerprint" of whale sharks?

   ⓐ so they could work with NASA's program

   ⓑ so they could measure the length of a whale shark

   ⓒ so they could track how much plankton a whale shark can suck up

   ⓓ so they could know if they were seeing the same individual over and over

3. What was NASA's program first used for?

   ⓐ to locate stars

   ⓑ to identify stars

   ⓒ to fingerprint stars

   ⓓ to count the number of stars

4. The title of this story is "A Whale of a Fish." This title was probably used because the story is about

   ⓐ a fish.

   ⓑ a kind of whale.

   ⓒ a fish the size of a whale.

   ⓓ a fish with a unique pattern on its back.

5. Think about how the word *unique* relates to *common*. What two words relate in the same way?

   | unique : common |

   ⓐ tip : end

   ⓑ broad : wide

   ⓒ clever : smart

   ⓓ colossal : small

Saving Richard Herrick

These are new words to practice.
Say each word 10 times.

✳ kidney	✳ vital
✳ organ	✳ transplant
✳ function	✳ ethics
✳ regulate	✳ benefit

Before or after reading the story, write one sentence that contains at least one new word.

_____

_____

_____

_____

Saving Richard Herrick

Richard Herrick was dying. He was only 23 years old. Richard's kidneys were not working. People are born with two kidneys. Kidneys are reddish-brown organs. An organ is a part of an animal or plant that is made of similar cells or tissues and performs a particular function, or purpose. The heart, liver, and lung are all different organs.

Kidneys have three important jobs. The first job is to regulate, or to control, the amount of water in the body. The second job is to produce vital hormones. When something is vital, it is necessary. The third job is to remove liquid waste from the body. It does this by taking extra water, salt, and waste from the blood to make urine. Richard's kidneys were so damaged that they were not functioning. They were unable to regulate the amount of water in his body or make urine.

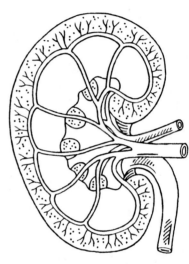

kidney

The year was 1954. At that time, no one had ever transplanted a human kidney. A kidney from one person had never been put into another person. Dr. Joseph Murray was willing to try. Dr. Murray knew that Richard's body would reject another person's kidney, but Richard had an identical twin. Dr. Murray thought that because the twins were identical, Richard's brother would not reject the transplant.

Before the surgery took place, there was a serious question to be answered. The question dealt with ethics. Ethics deals with what is right and wrong. If Dr. Murray removed the Richard's twin's kidney, he was doing something for the first time in medical history. He was doing major surgery on a normal, healthy person. The surgery was not for the healthy person's benefit, or good. Was the surgery ethical? Was it right?

People agreed that the surgery was ethical. The surgery was a success. Richard's life was saved. Today, thanks to Dr. Murray, many people have had successful kidney transplants. New drugs have helped people to benefit from the surgery. This is because the new drugs help people's bodies to accept the new kidneys even if they are not identical.

Saving Richard Herrick

After reading the story, answer the questions.
Fill in the circle next to the correct answer.

1. This story is mainly about

(a) what kidneys do.

(b) Dr. Murray and ethics.

(c) the first kidney transplant.

(d) Richard and his identical twin.

2. The kidney is not responsible for which job?

(a) producing vital hormones

(b) accepting transplanted organs

(c) regulating the amount of water in the body

(d) removing liquid body waste by making urine

3. Think about how the word *benefit* relates to *help*. What two words relate in the same way?

| benefit : help |

(a) organ : kidney

(b) ethical : wrong

(c) vital : necessary

(d) identical : different

4. What answer below is a question dealing with ethics?

(a) Is it okay to read a book during recess?

(b) Is it okay to skip breakfast in the morning?

(c) Is it okay to stay up late and watch a movie?

(d) Is it okay to steal medicine for a sick person?

5. From the story, you can tell that

(a) doctors do not care about ethics.

(b) people need only one functioning kidney.

(c) the liver and heart are the same type of organ.

(d) kidney transplants are done only on identical twins.

Dressing for Survival

These are new words to practice.

Say each word 10 times.

* survive	* pressurizes
* impaired	* vacuum
* unconscious	* undergarment
* independent	* tubing

Before or after reading the story, write one sentence that contains at least one new word.

_____

_____

_____

_____

Dressing for Survival

How long could one live if one were lost in space without a spacesuit? One would not survive long. The longest one might expect to live is four minutes. At first, one would feel light-headed. One would have impaired vision. When something is impaired, it is weak or damaged. One would have slurred speech. One would have loss of feeling. One would suffer all off these effects because of a lack of oxygen. Within 15 to 20 seconds, one would become unconscious. One would pass out.

One scientist said, "For a spacewalking astronaut to survive, a spacesuit must do something. It must turn the astronaut into an independent spacecraft. The independent spacecraft must protect the astronaut. It must also provide freedom of movement."

The spacesuit provides oxygen so that the astronaut does not become unconscious. It also removes the carbon dioxide the astronaut breathes out. The oxygen supply also pressurizes the suit. It is important that the suit be pressurized. If the suit were not pressurized, the astronaut's blood would boil. This is because space is a vacuum.

On Earth, there is air pressure. All the gases in the air press down on us. In the vacuum of space, there is no air pressing down. Water boils at a lower temperature when the air pressure is low. In the vacuum of space, the water in our bodies can begin to boil within seconds!

The spacesuit must also protect the astronaut from cold and heat. Temperatures can go down to -250°F (-157°C). They can rise to 250°F (121°C). To help stay cool, an astronaut wears a special undergarment underneath his or her suit. The undergarment contains 300 feet (91 m) of thin tubing. Water pumped through the tubing keeps the astronaut cool. An astronaut also wears a urine-collection device underneath a suit. The urine-collection device is not for survival. It is so a much needed bathroom break does not force an astronaut to cut a spacewalk short!

Dressing for Survival

After reading the story, answer the questions.
Fill in the circle next to the correct answer.

1. What is not listed as an effect of lack of oxygen?

   a. weak fingers
   b. slurred speech
   c. impaired vision
   d. loss of feeling

2. Why does an astronaut wear an undergarment containing tubing?

   a. so water can cool the astronaut
   b. so carbon dioxide can be removed
   c. so oxygen can pressurize the suit
   d. so freedom of movement can be provided

3. This story is mainly about

   a. what a vacuum is.
   b. what scientists say.
   c. what astronauts wear.
   d. what happens when there is a lack of oxygen.

4. At what place would water boil at the lowest temperature?

   a. in a valley
   b. at sea level
   c. under the ocean
   d. high on top of a mountain

5. Think about how the word *impaired* relates to *perfect*. What two words relate in the same way?

impaired : perfect

   a. begin : start
   b. survive : live
   c. temperature : cold
   d. underneath : above

Two to Trigger

These are new words to practice.
Say each word 10 times.

✳ lobe	✳ nutrients
✳ hinge	✳ bog
✳ carnivorous	✳ nitrogen
✳ photosynthesis	✳ trigger

Before or after reading the story, write one sentence that contains at least one new word.

_____

_____

_____

_____

Two to Trigger

The leaves of the Venus flytrap have two wing-like lobes. A lobe is a rounded part that sticks out. The lobes are joined with a hinge that allows the lobes to snap shut and then reopen. Three to four short hairs grow on the inside of each lobe. Touch one of these hairs, and nothing happens. Touch two of these hairs, and a meal may be in the making! What is going on?

A Venus flytrap is a carnivorous plant. When something is carnivorous, it eats meat. Green plants make their own food in a process called *photosynthesis*. Photosynthesis is the process in which the plant changes the sun's light energy to chemical energy. In photosynthesis, carbon dioxide in the air and water are used to produce glucose, a type of sugar. Plants also require nutrients. Most plants get the nutrients they need from soil and water.

Venus flytraps live in bogs in the southeast United States. A bog is a place with wet, spongy ground. It is a poorly drained wetland. Bogs have soil poor in nutrients, especially nitrogen. By being carnivorous, Venus flytraps are able to survive in bogs. They obtain, or get, the nitrogen and other nutrients they need by eating meat.

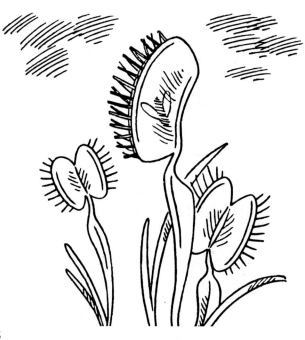

Venus flytrap

The Venus flytrap uses its hinged leaves as its trap. Insects are attracted to the trap by its color and the sweet smell of nectar. When an insect crawls onto the trap, the two lobes snap shut, trapping the insect inside. The plant then releases digestive juices, and the insect is dissolved into a nutrient-rich liquid. The plant obtains the nutrients it needs from the liquid.

The short hairs growing on the inside of the wing-like leaf lobes are trigger hairs. Touching one hair does not trigger, or set off, the trap—but touching two does. This is because a plant spends energy snapping shut its trap. It takes energy and time to reopen it. A plant does not want to waste energy. Live prey is more likely to set off two trigger hairs than a piece of grass or leaf.

Two to Trigger

After reading the story, answer the questions.
Fill in the circle next to the correct answer.

1. This story is mainly about

   ⓐ plants.

   ⓑ a carnivorous plant.

   ⓒ energy and green plants.

   ⓓ how plants get nutrients.

2. In photosynthesis, what does the plant produce?

   ⓐ glucose

   ⓑ nutrients

   ⓒ light energy

   ⓓ carbon dioxide

3. Why do Venus flytraps need to eat meat?

   ⓐ They need it for photosynthesis.

   ⓑ They live in nutrient-poor soil.

   ⓒ They spend energy snapping shut its trap.

   ⓓ They release digestive juices to dissolve it.

4. What part of your body has a lobe?

   ⓐ your arm

   ⓑ your leg

   ⓒ your eye

   ⓓ your ear

5. Think about how the word *trigger* relates to *start*. What two words relate in the same way?

> **trigger : start**

   ⓐ obtain : get

   ⓑ shut : reopen

   ⓒ eat : dissolve

   ⓓ change : produce

An Expedition for Bloodsuckers

These are new words to practice.

Say each word 10 times.

✴ expedition	✴ proboscis
✴ proposed	✴ lure
✴ zoologist	✴ successful
✴ leeches	✴ submerged

Before or after reading the story, write one sentence that contains at least one new word.

_____

_____

_____

_____

An Expedition
for Bloodsuckers

An expedition was proposed. An expedition is a long journey. The expedition was proposed, or suggested, in 1976 by a zoologist named Roy T. Sawyer. A zoologist studies animals, and Sawyer was an expert on leeches. Leeches are bloodsuckers. Leeches are found in all kinds of habitats, or places. They are found where it is cold, hot, wet, or dry. Sawyer knew about leeches that lived in the noses of camels. He knew about cave leeches that sucked the blood of bats. He knew about leeches that attacked the armpits of turtles.

Sawyer proposed an expedition to find a leech he had only heard about. The leech was enormous, with a six-inch long proboscis. A proboscis is a needle-like tube. Sawyer had heard that the leech inserted its proboscis into mammals to feed. Sawyer knew that most leeches used teeth to attach onto their hosts. They did not have proboscises. The few leeches Sawyer knew about with proboscises did not feed on mammals.

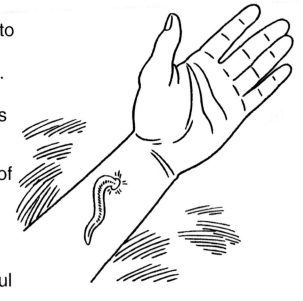

Sawyer took a team to the coastal marshes of French Guinea. French Guinea is a country in South America. Sawyer and other team members waded into the water bare-legged. They hoped to lure, or attract, leeches using their own flesh! The men were not successful luring any leeches where they first looked. They moved to a new marshy place, where once again they were prepared to lure leeches with their own flesh.

The men found a submerged boat at the new place. When something is submerged, it is under water. The men rolled the boat over. Something dark swam out from the submerged boat, and a team member grabbed it. It was the giant Amazon leech! It was 18 inches (46 cm) long! The man flung it up on the shore.

Sawyer picked it up and found that hundreds of tiny baby leeches were attached to its belly! Dozens of the babies fell onto Sawyer's hands! Sawyer had to call for help so he could get them off before they had time to attach. The expedition was successful. The team collected a total of 35 giant leeches for study.

An Expedition for Bloodsuckers

After reading the story, answer the questions.
Fill in the circle next to the correct answer.

1. What happened first after the men turned the boat over?

   ⓐ Sawyer had to call for help.

   ⓑ The men went into the water.

   ⓒ The giant leech was flung up on shore.

   ⓓ Something dark swam out from under it.

2. This story is mainly about

   ⓐ leeches around the world.

   ⓑ an expedition for leeches.

   ⓒ how the giant leech was caught.

   ⓓ a zoologist who studies leeches.

3. How many places did Sawyer's team go to find the giant leeches?

   ⓐ 1

   ⓑ 2

   ⓒ 3

   ⓓ 4

4. Think about how the word *ask* relates to *question*. What words relate in the same way?

ask : question

   ⓐ lure : catch

   ⓑ submerged : water

   ⓒ propose : suggest

   ⓓ proboscis : insert

5. Pick the word that best fills in the blank: _____ by the light, the moth flew into the trap.

   ⓐ Lured

   ⓑ Caught

   ⓒ Proposed

   ⓓ Submerged

All About Feet

These are new words to practice.
Say each word 10 times.

* fluid   * organ

* circulate   * function

* expanded   * sensitive

* chilly   * reduce

Before or after reading the story, write one sentence that contains at least one new word.

_____

_____

_____

_____

All About Feet

Juan's shoes fit perfectly when he took them off. When he put them back on two hours later they were too small. A short time later they fit again. How was this possible? Our bodies are filled with fluids, or liquids. Some fluids, such as blood, circulate. When something circulates it moves from place to place. Our blood circulates through the body from the heart.

When Juan removed his shoes, he sat down. During the hours Juan sat, his feet swelled up or expanded. When something expands, it grows bigger or wider. Juan's feet expanded because body fluids collected at his lowest point. As Juan was sitting, his feet were his lowest point. The fluids collecting in Juan's feet started moving quickly again once Juan was up and walking. With circulation back to normal, Juan's swollen feet shrank back to their normal size.

Juan went outside to ride his sled in the snow. Juan dressed for the chilly weather. He made sure to put on warm, thick socks. Even with the warm, thick socks, Juan's toes were the first part of his body to feel cold. Why did Juan's toes feel chilly first?

Each one of our organs—such as the heart, kidney, and liver—are made of special cells and tissues. Each organ has a particular function, or job. Our organs are very sensitive. When something is very sensitive, it is quick to change or react when acted on by something. Our organs are sensitive to cold. When our organs are too cold, they cannot function or perform their job properly.

Juan's toes felt the chill first because his body was protecting his organs. Body heat is easily lost through ones toes, fingers, ears, and nose. To reduce, or lessen heat loss, Juan's body reduced the amount of warm blood going to the places where heat is easily lost. By cutting down heat loss, Juan's body was working to protect his sensitive organs from the cold. With a reduced supply of warm blood circulating to his feet, Juan's toes were the first part of his body to feel the chill.

All About Feet

**After reading the story, answer the questions.
Fill in the circle next to the correct answer.**

1. What is not an organ?

   ⓐ hand
   ⓑ heart
   ⓒ liver
   ⓓ kidney

2. What might happen if one took his or her shoes off during a long airplane flight?

   ⓐ one's shoes might shrink
   ⓑ one's shoes might never fit again
   ⓒ one's shoes might feel loose after landing
   ⓓ one's shoes might feel tight after landing

3. This story is mainly about

   ⓐ why toes get cold.
   ⓑ what a boy named Juan did.
   ⓒ blood circulation and how it affects one's feet.
   ⓓ how sensitive organs are protected.

4. From the story, one can tell that it is most likely that

   ⓐ Juan lives where it snows a lot.
   ⓑ our blood circulates from the brain.
   ⓒ the kidney is the most sensitive organ.
   ⓓ there are no important organs in our toes.

5. Think about how the word *expand* relates to *reduce*. What two words relate in the same way?

   | expand : reduce |

   ⓐ chill : cool
   ⓑ swell : shrink
   ⓒ circulate : move
   ⓓ perform : protect

Surviving Without a Head

These are new words to practice.

Say each word 10 times.

* survive   * spiracle

* exoskeleton   * scavenger

* scattered   * antennae

* obtain   * segment

Before or after reading the story, write one sentence that contains at least one new word.

_____

_____

_____

_____

Surviving Without a Head

There is an animal that has been present on Earth for a long time. The animal can live up to two years, but its kind has been present for more than 400 million years. When the head of this animal is cut off, the animal does not die immediately. It can survive for up to one week. When the animal finally dies, it does not die because its head was cut off. It dies of thirst. What in the world could this animal be?

The animal is the cockroach. Cockroaches are winged insects. Like all adult insects, cockroaches have six legs. Unlike people, cockroaches do not have inner skeletons. Instead of a skeleton inside the body to support it, cockroaches have exoskeletons. An exoskeleton is a tough outer covering. The cockroach's exoskeleton supports and protects its body.

Unlike people, a cockroach's brain is not all in one place. A cockroach's brain is scattered, or spread, along the underside of its body. A cockroach does not die when its head is removed because of its scattered brain. When a cockroach's head is cut off, the cockroach does not lose all of its brain. There is enough brain left along the underside of the cockroach's body for it to survive.

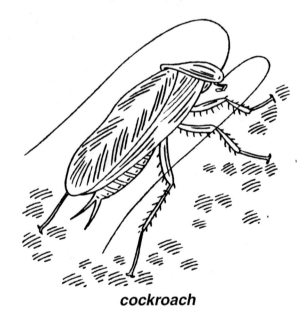

cockroach

Cockroaches do not obtain, or get, air the same way people do. Cockroaches obtain air through spiracles. Spiracles are tiny holes. A cockroach's spiracles are not located on its head. They are located on the sides of its body. There are over 4,000 different kinds of cockroaches. Most cockroaches live in warm, wet places.

Cockroaches are scavengers. A scavenger feeds on garbage. It feeds on dead or rotting animals and plants. Cockroaches use their antennae to help them scavenge, or search for, food. A cockroach's antennae are located on its head. The antennae are made up of about 100 segments, or parts. The antennae bend well because of the number of segments they are made up of. A cockroach uses its antennae to smell rotting food. It uses its antennae to feel vibrations, or movement. It uses its antennae to sense temperature.

Surviving Without a Head

After reading the story, answer the questions.
Fill in the circle next to the correct answer.

1. A cockroach can survive when its head is removed because

   (a) it gets air through spiracles.

   (b) it uses its antennae to smell rotting food.

   (c) it has an exoskeleton to support and protect it.

   (d) its brain is scattered along the underside of its body.

2. Which is made up of segments?

   (a) a banana

   (b) an apple

   (c) an orange

   (d) a watermelon

3. This story is mainly about

   (a) brains.

   (b) insects.

   (c) scavengers.

   (d) cockroaches.

4. From the story, one can tell that

   (a) no insects are scavengers.

   (b) all insects are scavengers.

   (c) some insects are scavengers.

   (d) only insects are scavengers.

5. Think about how the word *skeleton* relates to *exoskeleton*. What two words relate in the same way?

   | skeleton : exoskeleton |

   (a) warm : wet

   (b) inside : outside

   (d) rotting : animal

   (c) scattered : underside

The Substance Answer

These are new words to practice.
Say each word 10 times.

✳ substance	✳ chlorine
✳ sodium	✳ dissolve
✳ symbol	✳ salary
✳ explosion	✳ statues

**Before or after reading the story, write one sentence
that contains at least one new word.**

_____

_____

_____

_____

The Substance Answer

An old riddle goes, "Throw this rock into the water, and it will change into water. What is it?" The answer to this riddle is a kind of substance. A substance is something you can touch and see. Everything around you is made from substances. Substances are made from elements. Elements are substances made of only one type of atom. An atom is very small. An atom is the smallest amount of an element that has all the properties of that element.

What two elements make up the riddle answer substance? One element is sodium. The symbol for sodium is Na. If you add sodium to water, it produces an explosion! The second element is chlorine. The symbol for chlorine is Cl. Chlorine is a poisonous gas. The two elements alone do not answer the question, but putting them together does.

Together, the two elements make ordinary table salt! Ordinary salt does not produce an explosion when it is put in water. It does not produce a poisonous gas. What salt does do in water is dissolve. When a solid dissolves, it turns into a liquid.

Long ago, salt was so valuable that it cost as much as gold. It was put on meat and fish to keep them from becoming rotten. Roman soldiers received salt as part of their pay. The Latin word *salarium* means "salt money." Today, our word "salary" comes from this Latin word. A salary is one's pay. It is a fixed amount of money paid at regular times for work done.

Most salt comes from oceans or places where salty water has dried up, but some salt is mined and dug out of the earth. One mine in Poland is over 700 years old. Miners have dug 100 miles (30 m) of tunnels more than 300 feet (91 m) under the ground. They have carved out a salt church filled with salt statues of holy men and women. One can visit this salt church today and see the statues. One can also visit a tall, carved-out salt room that has been used for bungee jumping!

The Substance Answer

After reading the story, answer the questions.
Fill in the circle next to the correct answer.

1. This story is mainly about

(a) a mine.
(b) a riddle.
(c) an element.
(d) a substance.

2. What symbol below means salt?

(a) NC
(b) NaCl
(c) SaCl
(d) SoCl

3. What answer below lists the words in the order of the smallest piece to the largest?

(a) element, atom, substance
(b) atom, element, substance
(c) substance, element, atom
(d) atom, substance, element

4. The best explanation below for why salt may not be as valuable today is that

(a) we have computers.
(b) we have telephones.
(c) we have televisions.
(d) we have refrigerators.

5. Think about how the word *riddle* relates to *question*. What two words relate in the same way?

riddle : question

(a) song : tune
(b) story : letter
(c) book : chapter
(d) poem : newspaper

56   ©Teacher Created Resources, Inc.

The "She" in the Tongue Twister

These are new words to practice.
Say each word 10 times.

* poverty	* specimen
* fossils	* frequent
* Jurassic	* skeleton
* prehistoric	* excavated

Before or after reading the story, write one sentence that contains at least one new word.

_____

_____

_____

_____

The "She" in the Tongue Twister

"She sells seashells down by the seashore" is a tongue twister. Try to say it five times fast. It is very difficult. Many people believe that there is a real person behind this tongue twister. The people believe that the "she" is Mary Anning.

Mary was born in England. She was born into poverty. Poverty is the condition of being poor. It is the condition of not having enough to live on. Mary's father was a carpenter, but his work did not pay enough for his family to live on. To help buy food and clothes, Mary's father looked for and sold fossils. A fossil is the hardened remains or prints of animals or plants.

Mary lived in a place with high sea cliffs filled with fossils from the Jurassic Period. Scientists believe that the Jurassic Period was an age of reptiles. It occurred 195 to 140 million years ago. When Mary was growing up in the early 1800s, scientists were just learning that fossils were the remains of prehistoric creatures. When something is prehistoric, it is of the time before history was written. Scientists and museums were willing to pay for fossil specimens. A specimen is a part of a whole or one thing of a group.

When Mary was only 11, her father died. To keep the family from starving, Mary had to find fossils. It was dangerous work. Loose rocks often fell. Worse, there were frequent rockslides. When something is frequent, it happens a lot. Mary lost her dog in one rockslide when an entire wall of a cliff came crashing down. Still, she did not quit.

When Mary was only 12, she found and excavated the first complete skeleton of an ichthyosaur. When something is excavated, it is uncovered. It is dug out. It took Mary a year to excavate the skeleton. It was the first complete skeleton that the Geological Society in London had ever seen. Over the years, Mary's fame grew. She discovered many new specimens of prehistoric creatures. In 1838, Mary was officially recognized for all that she had done for science.

The "She" in the Tongue Twister

**After reading the story, answer the questions.
Fill in the circle next to the correct answer.**

1. When was the Jurassic Period?

   ⓐ in the early 1800s

   ⓑ 11 to 12 million years ago

   ⓒ 195 to 140 million years ago

   ⓓ 1838 to 140 million years ago

2. This story is mainly about

   ⓐ a tongue twister.

   ⓑ a girl who helped her family.

   ⓒ the dangers of collecting fossils.

   ⓓ the first complete ichthyosaur skeleton.

3. Which word best completes this sentence: "I had to _____ my shoe after my dog buried it."

   ⓐ fossil

   ⓑ poverty

   ⓒ excavate

   ⓓ specimen

4. Think about how the word *frequent* relates to *often*. What two words relate in the same way?

   | frequent : often |

   ⓐ fast : slow

   ⓑ old : young

   ⓒ tall : short

   ⓓ big : enormous

5. Why might some people think Mary is the "she" in the tongue twister "She sells seashells at the seashore"?

   ⓐ Mary sold fossils she found on cliffs by the sea.

   ⓑ Mary excavated the complete skeleton of an ichthyosaur.

   ⓒ Mary lived during the Jurassic Period in prehistoric times.

   ⓓ Mary was recognized in 1838 for all that she had done for science.

Two Strange Eruptions

These are new words to practice.
Say each word 10 times.

* bizarre	* carbon dioxide
* livestock	* erupted
* suffocation	* spew
* vent	* prevent

Before or after reading the story, write one sentence that contains at least one new word.

_____

_____

_____

_____

Two Strange Eruptions

In 1986, there was a bizarre, or really strange, explosion. A lake blew up. 1,800 people and 3,500 livestock animals died from suffocation. Livestock animals are kept or raised on farms. Suffocation occurs when one does not have enough air to breathe. How could such a bizarre event take palace? The lake that blew up is in Cameroon, a country in Africa. The lake is called Lake Nyos.

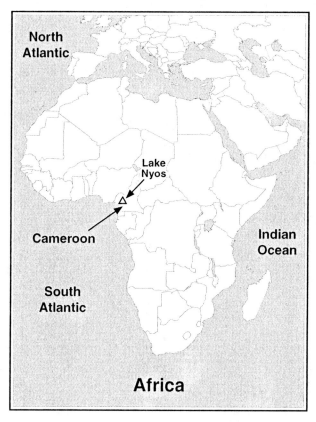

North Atlantic

Lake Nyos

Cameroon

Indian Ocean

South Atlantic

Africa

Lake Nyos sits on top of a volcanic vent. A vent is an opening, or passage, for something like air, gas, or molten rock to pass through or escape. What happened in Lake Nyos is that gases inside the Earth seeped from the vent into the lake. Over time, carbon dioxide and other gases built up in the water. When they reached a certain level, they erupted. An eruption is when something spews forth or spurts out forcefully. The eruption filled the air with a huge amount of carbon dioxide. Any living creature that breathed it in died.

Today scientists are working hard to prevent, or stop, another explosion. They have laid pipes from which gas can vent. The amount of gas vented is controlled so that it is only released, or let go, in small amounts. Releasing the gas slowly prevents a huge amount of carbon dioxide from building up.

A very different, but equally strange, eruption started on May 29, 2006. The bizarre eruption took place in Indonesia, a country in Asia. Miners were drilling for natural gas. After an accident in one well, hot mud began to spew through an opening. Every day, enough mud pours out to cover a football field about 75 feet (23 m) deep. Factories were covered in mud. Homes were swallowed. Rice fields were ruined. More than 10,000 people were forced to flee.

Scientists are looking for ways to stop the mud. They have found the place under the ground where it is coming from. Now they want to find a way to prevent its flow. Meanwhile, they are building dams. They are looking for places to pump the pools of mud collecting behind the dams.

Two Strange Eruptions

After reading the story, answer the questions.
Fill in the circle next to the correct answer.

1. This story is mainly about

ⓐ volcanic vents.

ⓑ a lake in Cameroon.

ⓒ two bizarre countries.

ⓓ spewing mud and gases.

2. Which animal below is not a livestock animal?

ⓐ cat

ⓑ pig

ⓒ goat

ⓓ chicken

3. Which statement is true?

ⓐ Indonesia is a country in Africa.

ⓑ Mud ruined rice fields in Cameroon.

ⓒ Dams were built to protect Lake Nyos.

ⓓ The lake exploded before the mud erupted.

4. What would be most bizarre thing to find in your desk?

ⓐ a live frog

ⓑ a big eraser

ⓒ a blue pencil

ⓓ an extra notebook

5. Think about how the word *prevent* relates to *allow*. What two words relate in the same way?

| **prevent : allow** |

ⓐ build : make

ⓑ glance : look

ⓒ release : trap

ⓓ erupt : explode

A Parasite's Greatest Enemy

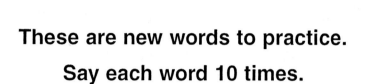

These are new words to practice.
Say each word 10 times.

* parasite	* scolex
* host	* segments
* intestines	* microscopic
* digestive	* interlock

Before or after reading the story, write one sentence that contains at least one new word.

_____

_____

_____

_____

A Parasite's Greatest Enemy

It never stops growing. It can reach a length of 60 feet (18 m) in its 30-year lifespan. It doesn't have legs, bones, teeth, claws, eyes, or ears. It doesn't have a stomach or intestines. Yet it is alive and can do humans serious harm. What is it? It is a tapeworm. The tapeworm is a parasite. A parasite lives on and feeds off a host. A host can be a plant or animal.

Tapeworms live and grow in the intestines of people and animals. Intestines are part of the digestive system. They are the coiled tubes below the stomach where digestion is finished. The tapeworm body has a scolex, neck, and segments. The scolex is made up of hooks and suckers that are used to attach to the host's intestines.

Segments grow from the neck and form a long, soft, segmented ribbon. A segment is a section or part into which something can be separated. The segments are flat, narrow, and filled with microscopic, or very small, eggs. The segments are covered with "fingers" that interlock with its host's intestinal wall. When something is interlocked, it fits tightly together. Securely attached, the tapeworm soaks up nutrients directly from the host's digested food.

tapeworm

Tapeworms are hard to destroy. One can take a special medicine, but the best way to deal with them is to break their lifecycle. Tapeworms spread when segments break off and are passed out of the body in waste. One should always wash one's hands after going to the bathroom. This keeps one from spreading the microscopic eggs with one's hands.

A toilet is a probably a tapeworm's most dangerous enemy. This is because when waste is flushed away, it goes to a sewage-treatment plant. At the plant, the sewage is cleaned and purified. The eggs are destroyed. If waste is left on the ground or runs into water, animals can eat or drink the eggs. People can get tapeworms from eating infected animals. To keep from becoming infected, people must be careful to cook their meat properly.

A Parasite's Greatest Enemy

**After reading the story, answer the questions.
Fill in the circle next to the correct answer.**

1. This story is mainly about

   (a) a host.

   (b) an enemy.

   (c) an animal.

   (d) a parasite.

2. Why do you think most tapeworm problems happen in poor countries?

   (a) People do not cook their food.

   (b) The microscopic eggs cannot be seen.

   (c) The lifecycle of the tapeworm is broken.

   (d) There are fewer toilets and sewage-treatment plants.

3. Think about how the word *parasite* relates to *host*. What two words relate in the same way?

parasite : host

   (a) flea : dog

   (b) lion : zebra

   (c) tick : blood

   (d) fish : shark

4. From the story, you can tell that

   (a) parasites are easy to destroy.

   (b) washing one's hands is very important.

   (c) the tapeworm needs to digest its food.

   (d) only humans can be infected with tapeworms.

5. About how long can a tapeworm grow?

   (a) as long as a bus

   (b) as long as a desk

   (c) as long as a bike

   (d) as long as a pencil

What Color Was the Bear?

These are new words to practice.

Say each word 10 times.

* conundrum   * constructed

* soundly   * siblings

* logically   * identical

* conclusion   * seal

Before or after reading the story, write one sentence that contains at least one new word.

_____

_____

_____

_____

What Color Was the Bear?

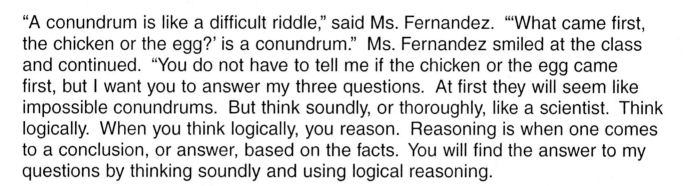

"A conundrum is like a difficult riddle," said Ms. Fernandez. "'What came first, the chicken or the egg?' is a conundrum." Ms. Fernandez smiled at the class and continued. "You do not have to tell me if the chicken or the egg came first, but I want you to answer my three questions. At first they will seem like impossible conundrums. But think soundly, or thoroughly, like a scientist. Think logically. When you think logically, you reason. Reasoning is when one comes to a conclusion, or answer, based on the facts. You will find the answer to my questions by thinking soundly and using logical reasoning.

"My first question is about a bear. The Millers constructed, or built, a house. Every wall in the Millers' house faced south. After the house was constructed, the Millers looked out the window and saw a bear. What color was the bear?

"My second question is about Jack and Jon. Jack and Jon were siblings. Siblings are people with at least one common parent. Jack and Jon were brothers. They had the same parents. They looked identical, and they were the same age. But Jack and Jon were not twins! How could this be possible?

"My third question is about Ben. Ben decided to wash the dishes and filled the sink with water. When Ben tried to turn the water off, the faucet fell off! The water continued to pour out. The kitchen door was closed with an airtight seal, and Ben couldn't get it open. The windows were sealed tightly, too. How did Ben stop the water from overflowing and filling up the room?"

Using logical reasoning and sound thinking, the class came to the correct conclusions. For question one, they knew that for all the walls of the house to face south, the house had to be built on the North Pole. Only white polar bears live in the far North. For the second question, they concluded that Jack and Jon had at least one other brother just like them, and together they were identical triplets. For the final question, they concluded that all Ben had to do was pull the plug in the sink's drain.

What Color Was the Bear?

After reading the story, answer the questions.
Fill in the circle next to the correct answer.

1. Using the same reasoning as in the story, a house with all its walls facing north must be built

   (a) with windows.

   (b) on the South Pole.

   (c) on the North Pole.

   (d) where polar bears live.

2. When something is closed tightly, it is

   (a) sealed.

   (b) logical.

   (c) identical.

   (d) constructed.

3. This story is mainly about

   (a) where polar bears live.

   (b) thinking logically to find three conclusions.

   (c) finding out if the chicken or the egg came first.

   (d) Ms. Fernandez showing children what scientists do.

4. If a house is soundly constructed, it is most likely

   (a) built on wet sand.

   (b) built on sticky mud.

   (c) built on frozen snow.

   (d) built on solid ground.

5. Think about how the word *sister* relates to *sibling*. What two words relate in the same way?

sister : sibling

   (a) mother : son

   (b) aunt : niece

   (c) father : parent

   (d) grandmother : brother

A Different Walk

These are new words to practice.
Say each word 10 times.

∗ giraffe	∗ relative
∗ rear	∗ vertebrae
∗ stride	∗ predator
∗ merely	∗ defend

Before or after reading the story, write one sentence that contains at least one new word.

_____

_____

_____

_____

A Different Walk

Picture in your head a dog or cat walking. Think about how it moves its legs. Now, picture a giraffe. Giraffes do not walk like most other four-footed animals. Giraffes swing both legs on one side of the body forward at the same time. This means that they swing the front and back, or rear, legs on the left side forward together. Then they swing the front and rear right legs forward together. Why do giraffes walk differently than most other four-footed animals?

Giraffes are the tallest land animals in the world. The height of an average male is about 17 feet (5.2 m). An average female measures about 14 feet (4.3 m). Much of a giraffe's height comes from its legs and neck. A giraffe's long legs means that it has a very long stride, or step. When a giraffe is merely, or only, walking, its strides are 15 feet (4.6 m) long!

A giraffe has a short body relative, or compared, to its legs. The length of a giraffe's legs and stride relative to its short body is why a giraffe needs to walk differently than most other four-footed animals. If a giraffe walked like other animals, its rear feet would be stepping on its front feet all the time! Merely walking would be cause enough for a giraffe to trip over itself!

We have seven vertebrae, or bones, in our necks. A giraffe's neck can measure over 6.5 feet (2 m) long—but it has only seven vertebrae, too. Of course, its vertebrae are much bigger! A giraffe's vertebrae can be over 10 inches (25 cm) high. Because of its long legs, a giraffe's neck is not long enough to reach down to the ground. To drink, a giraffe must spread its front legs open wide or bend its knees.

A predator attacks other animals. Most predators leave giraffes alone because of their size. Sometimes predators, like lions, will attack a baby giraffe. A mother giraffe will defend its young by kicking out with its legs. Mother giraffes have been known to kick the heads off of lions while defending their babies!

A Different Walk

**After reading the story, answer the questions.
Fill in the circle next to the correct answer.**

1. How many vertebrae are in a giraffe's neck?

   ⓐ 6
   ⓑ 7
   ⓒ 14
   ⓓ 25

2. This story is mainly about

   ⓐ giraffe legs.
   ⓑ a long stride.
   ⓒ how animals walk.
   ⓓ giraffe predators.

3. Why doesn't a giraffe walk like most other four-footed animals?

   ⓐ it is the tallest land animal
   ⓑ it has to spread its legs to drink
   ⓒ its back legs would step on its front legs
   ⓓ its legs are strong enough to kick the head off a lion

4. Think about how the word *defend* relates to *attack*. What two words relate in the same way?

   | defend : attack |

   ⓐ rear : front
   ⓑ predator : lion
   ⓒ vertebrae : bone
   ⓓ different : together

5. Pick the word below that best completes the sentence: "Don't expect her to walk far. She is _only_ a child."

   ⓐ sadly
   ⓑ truly
   ⓒ merely
   ⓓ finally

A Spy or an Alien?

These are new words to practice.
Say each word 10 times.

* cosmonaut   * ejected

* atmosphere   * parachuted

* orbited   * alien

* hatch   * capsule

Before or after reading the story, write one sentence that contains at least one new word.

_____

_____

_____

_____

A Spy or an Alien?

Yuri Gagarin was a Russian cosmonaut. In Russia, astronauts are called cosmonauts. On April 12, 1961, Gagarin rocketed out of Earth's atmosphere. He entered space. Gagarin was the first man to leave Earth's atmosphere. He was the first man to enter space. Once in space, Gagarin orbited, or circled, the Earth. He orbited at a speed of over 17,000 miles (27,200 km) per hour. Gagarin's trip took a total of 108 minutes.

On his return, the hatch of Gagarin's ship blew open. A hatch is an opening in a ship deck or floor. Gagarin was ejected, or thrown out. When Gagarin was ejected, he was 4.3 miles (6.9 km) above the Earth. Gagarin parachuted down to Earth. He landed safely.

Gagarin landed near a small village. People came to greet him. The people first thought Gagarin was a spy. They thought he had come from America. Then some of the people became afraid. They thought Gagarin might be an alien. An alien was much worse than a spy. A spy would have come only from America. An alien would have come from outer space!

Yuri Gagarin

Gagarin was asked if he had parachuted down from outer space. "As a matter of fact," Gagarin replied, "I have!" Gagarin then explained that he was a cosmonaut. Gagarin became a hero. He became famous all over Russia. He became famous all over the world. Gagarin was living proof that science could take mankind out of this world.

Why was Gagarin chosen to be first? Many other test pilots wanted to be cosmonauts, too. The first space capsule was very small. Gagarin was very short. Gagarin was so short that he sat on a cushion when he flew jets. The choice was between Gagarin and another short test pilot because they could fit in the capsule. Oddly enough, the final choice came down to hair. Gagarin was picked to be first because he had the plainest hairstyle. Gagarin was told only five days before blast off that he would be first.

A Spy or an Alien?

After reading the story, answer the questions.
Fill in the circle next to the correct answer.

1. This story is mainly about

ⓐ the first man in space.

ⓑ why Gagarin was chosen.

ⓒ how long the space trip was.

ⓓ what people thought about Gagarin.

2. From the story, you can tell that Gagarin was

ⓐ the best test pilot in Russia.

ⓑ shorter than most test pilots.

ⓒ willing to live in a different world.

ⓓ the only test pilot with a plain hairstyle.

3. Which statement is false?

ⓐ Gagarin was a Russian cosmonaut.

ⓑ Gagarin was ejected when the hatch blew open.

ⓒ The people in the village knew Gagarin was coming.

ⓓ No one had left Earth's atmosphere before Gagarin.

4. How many days before leaving did Gagarin find out that he was going to be first in space?

ⓐ one day

ⓑ five days

ⓒ seven days

ⓓ eleven days

5. Think about how the word *alien* relates to *strange*. What two words relate in the same way?

alien : strange

ⓐ first : last

ⓑ hatch : open

ⓒ short : tall

ⓓ famous : known

Why Pig Bristles Were Glued on Ants

These are new words to practice.

Say each word 10 times.

* extended   * route

* bristle   * observe

* extremely   * internal

* terrain   * pedometer

Before or after reading the story, write one sentence that contains at least one new word.

_____

_____

_____

_____

Why Pig Bristles Were Glued on Ants

One scientist carefully extended ants' legs. When something is extended, it is made longer. The scientist extended the ants' legs by gluing pig bristles on to them. A bristle is a short, stiff, prickly hair. Why would a scientist extend ants' legs with pig bristles?

The scientist was studying ants that live in the Sahara desert. The Sahara desert is the largest desert in the world. It is on the continent of Africa. From east to west, it runs from the Atlantic Ocean to the Red Sea. From north to south, it stretches down around 1,200 miles (1,920 km). It gets extremely hot in the Sahara. In the daytime, it gets hot enough to fry an egg on the sand. High temperatures can go over 136°F (58°C). On winter nights, it can get extremely cold. Temperatures can fall below freezing.

To find food, the Saharan ants have to leave their nests and travel across the flat desert terrain, or land. Despite turns, twists, and terrain without landmarks, when it comes time for the ants to head home, they do not retrace their steps. They head home by the shortest possible route.

The scientist knew that the ants used sunlight to figure out direction. But direction and distance are two different things. The scientist wanted to know how the ants always knew the shortest possible route. The scientist caught the ants at a feeder 30 feet (9 m) away from the ants' nest. There, the scientist extended some ants' legs. He shortened others. Then he observed, or watched, the ants returning to their nest. The ants' with the attached pig bristles overshot their nest! They went too far! The ants with shortened legs did not go far enough.

The observations proved to the scientist that the ants had an internal pedometer. A pedometer keeps track of distance covered. It keeps track by responding to body motion at each step. The ants' internal pedometer was part of their nervous system. It allowed them to measure the distance. Using their internal pedometer, the ants could figure out the shortest way home.

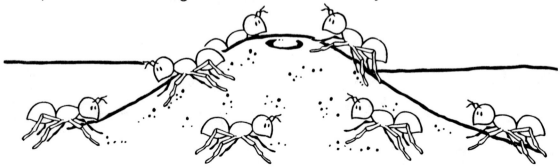

Why Pig Bristles Were Glued on Ants

After reading the story, answer the questions.
Fill in the circle next to the correct answer.

1. This story is mainly about

   ⓐ ants.

   ⓑ the Sahara desert.

   ⓒ using pig bristles.

   ⓓ how ants figure out distance.

2. Sarah always seems to know what time to get up in the morning. It is as if she has a(n) _____ alarm clock.

   ⓐ bristle

   ⓑ terrain

   ⓒ internal

   ⓓ observation

3. Think about how the word *extend* relates to *shorten*. What two words relate in the same way?

   | extend : shorten |

   ⓐ route : way

   ⓑ respond : ignore

   ⓒ pedometer : step

   ⓓ direction : north

4. The ants' with extended legs overshot their nest because

   ⓐ the sand temperature got extremely hot.

   ⓑ they needed to take more steps to get home.

   ⓒ they went a greater distance with each step.

   ⓓ they could not find their way without landmarks.

5. What is true about the Sahara?

   ⓐ Temperatures are too extreme for life.

   ⓑ You can fry an egg on the sand at night.

   ⓒ It runs east to west around 1,200 miles (1,920 km).

   ⓓ It stretches from the Atlantic Ocean to the Red Sea.

Getting Sick on Purpose

These are new words to practice.

Say each word 10 times.

* resuscitation   * researched

* revived   * microbe

* diagnose   * microorganism

* kerosene   * ulcer

Before or after reading the story, write one sentence that contains at least one new word.

_____

_____

_____

_____

Getting Sick on Purpose

Twelve-year-old Barry Marshall was babysitting. He found his 18-month-old sister choking. He quickly phoned emergency services. While waiting for the ambulance, he tried to practice mouth-to-mouth resuscitation. When one is resuscitated, one is brought back to life. One is revived.

Dr Barry Marshall

His sister did not need resuscitation, as she was still breathing. Still, Barry's attempt did help. Why? When Barry attempted resuscitation, he was able to diagnose, or figure out, what was wrong. When Barry's mouth was on his sister's, he smelt kerosene. Kerosene is a type of oil. It ended up that his sister had swallowed some kerosene that had been stored in a milk bottle.

Many years later, Barry swallowed something that made him very ill. Unlike his sister, who had not known what she was doing, Barry did it on purpose. Barry had become a doctor. One of his things he researched, or studied, was a spiral microbe. *Microbe* is another word for "microorganism." Microorganisms are so small that they can only be seen with a microscope. Barry believed that these spiral microbes caused stomach ulcers.

A stomach ulcer is an open sore in the stomach. It is incredibly painful. All over the world, people were suffering from stomach ulcers. They were taking lots of medicine. Many were being operated on. Some were even dying. There was no cure. Barry was sure that the spiral microbes were the cause. To cure a stomach ulcer, all one had to do was take some antibiotics to kill the spiral microbes. No one believed Barry. People refused to publish his research papers. He was openly laughed at.

To prove his point and get help to people who needed it, Barry infected himself. He drank a mixture filled with the spiral microbes. He was diagnosed with a stomach ulcer and very ill. Then, he treated himself with antibiotics and cured himself. In 2005, Barry shared the Nobel Prize with one of his fellow researchers for his work. The Nobel Prize is one of the most respected prizes in the world.

Getting Sick on Purpose

**After reading the story, answer the questions.
Fill in the circle next to the correct answer.**

1. Why didn't Barry's sister need resuscitation?

   (a) She was choking.

   (b) She was still breathing.

   (c) She was 18 months old.

   (d) She was in need of being revived.

2. From the story, you can tell that kerosene and other poisons should not be stored in bottles used for other things because people

   (a) might need mouth-to-mouth resuscitation.

   (b) might not know exactly how much they have.

   (c) might begin to choke and not get the proper diagnosis.

   (d) might accidentally swallow it thinking it is something else.

3. This story is mainly about

   (a) a diagnosis.

   (b) microorganisms.

   (c) a Nobel Prize winner.

   (d) mouth-to-mouth resuscitation.

4. What was Barry's purpose in drinking the spiral microbes?

   (a) He wanted to win the Nobel Prize.

   (b) He wanted people to stop laughing at him.

   (c) He wanted to see if he could make a diagnosis.

   (d) He wanted to show how people could be cured of ulcers.

5. Think about how the word *kerosene* relates to *oil*. What two words relate in the same way?

kerosene : oil

   (a) tree : oak

   (b) car : train

   (c) Dalmatian : dog

   (d) school : research

Where Days Are Different Lengths

These are new words to practice.
Say each word 10 times.

* rotate   * solar system

* axis   * gravity

* fusion   * orbit

* equator   * weight

**Before or after reading the story, write one sentence
that contains at least one new word.**

_____

_____

_____

_____

Where Days Are Different Lengths

On Earth, a day is 24 hours. That is how long it takes the Earth to rotate, or turn completely, on its axis. An axis is a real or imaginary line about which something turns. The Earth's axis passes between the North and South Poles. A day on the sun is not the same length as on the Earth. In fact, a day is not the same length at different places on the sun! How can this be?

Unlike the Earth, the sun does not have a solid crust. The sun is a fiery ball made of hot gases. It is mostly hydrogen and helium. The sun's energy comes from fusion. Fusion is a process that turns hydrogen into helium. One day, the sun will burn itself out—but that won't be for at least five billion years.

The sun's outer layer rotates more rapidly at the equator than at the poles. At the equator, it takes about the time of 25 Earth days to make a complete rotation, or turn. It takes longer for the sun's outer layers to make a complete turn at its poles. At the sun's poles, a day is about 30 Earth days long. This is because it takes about 30 Earth days to make a complete rotation, or spin.

The sun is the closest star and the only one we can see in the daytime. For a star, it is of average size, but it is the biggest thing in our solar system. It is wider than 100 Earths. Gravity is the invisible force that pulls objects toward the center of a planet or star. The sun's gravity is very strong because of its size. The sun's gravity keeps Earth and the other planets in our solar system in orbit. An orbit is a path followed by an object going around another.

Gravity affects our weight. If one weighed 100 pounds (45 kg) on Earth, would one have a bigger or smaller weight on the sun? One would weigh more because the pull of the sun's gravity is more powerful. One would weigh more than 5,500 pounds (2,497 kg)!

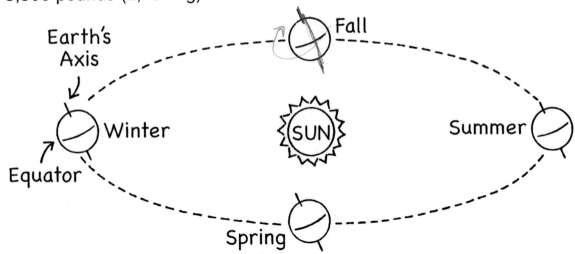

Where Days Are Different Lengths

**After reading the story, answer the questions.
Fill in the circle next to the correct answer.**

1. This story is mainly about

   ⓐ a star.

   ⓑ our solar system.

   ⓒ how long a day is.

   ⓓ what keeps us in orbit.

2. About how much longer is a day at the Sun's poles than at the equator?

   ⓐ 5 Earth days

   ⓑ 15 Earth days

   ⓒ 25 Earth days

   ⓓ 30 Earth days

3. Think about how the word *planet* relates to *sun*. What two words relate in the same way?

> **planet : sun**

   ⓐ star : sun

   ⓑ moon : planet

   ⓒ axis : equator

   ⓓ orbit : rotate

4. Astronauts who have landed on the moon weigh less on the moon than they do on Earth. This is because

   ⓐ the moon orbits the Earth.

   ⓑ the moon is farther from the sun.

   ⓒ the sun's gravity is much more powerful.

   ⓓ the moon's gravity is less than Earth's gravity.

5. What is the reason that the sun is the only star we can see during the day?

   ⓐ its size

   ⓑ it is much closer than other stars

   ⓒ its gravity

   ⓓ it is made of fiery gases

All About Smelling

These are new words to practice.

Say each word 10 times.

✳ scent	✳ cavity
✳ recognize	✳ nasal
✳ sensitive	✳ projecting
✳ olfactory	✳ detect

Before or after reading the story, write one sentence that contains at least one new word.

_____

_____

_____

_____

All About Smelling

A scent is a smell. When you smell something, you catch its scent. You get a hint of it. How many different scents do you think you can recognize, or identify? Most people can recognize about 4,000 different scents. Other people have extremely sensitive noses. They can recognize many more scents. They can identify up to 10,000 different smells!

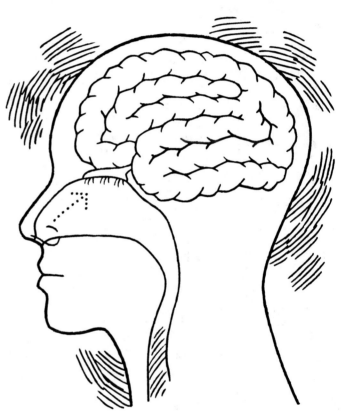

We are able to smell because of our olfactory cells. Each one of our nostrils leads back into a cavity. A cavity is a hole or hollow place. A patch of olfactory cells is found on the roof of each nasal cavity. Each patch is smaller than a postage stamp. There are about 10 million olfactory cells in each patch. We have about 20 million olfactory cells in total.

The olfactory cells are very sensitive. Each olfactory cell has between six and eight tiny hairs projecting, or sticking out, from it. The projecting hairs detect chemicals in the air. The chemicals in the air cause smells. Once the chemicals have been detected, the cells send the information to the brain.

Sometimes our sense of smell does not seem to work. For example, people with colds have a hard time smelling. This is because of mucus. Our bodies produce mucus when we have a cold. The mucus is produced to defend our nasal membranes. The mucus defends our nasal membranes against the cold virus. When a lot of mucus is produced, the nose gets blocked up. When the nose is blocked, chemicals in the air cannot reach the olfactory cells.

Our sense of smell is very closely tied to our sense of taste. It is hard to tell what one is eating if one cannot smell it. People usually find hot food to be tastier than cold food. This is because hot food releases more chemicals into the air than cold food. The olfactory cells detect the extra chemicals. The increased smell makes the food seem as if it has more taste.

All About Smelling

**After reading the story, answer the questions.
Fill in the circle next to the correct answer.**

1. This story is mainly about

  (a) olfactory cells.

  (b) our sense of smell.

  (c) when we have a cold.

  (d) how smell is tied to taste.

2. What might be a good job for someone with an extremely sensitive nose?

  (a) chef

  (b) pilot

  (c) farmer

  (d) teacher

3. Think about how the word *produce* relates to *make*. What two words relate in the same way?

> **produce : make**

  (a) detect : find

  (b) smell : taste

  (c) defend : project

  (d) recognize : release

4. Someone who can identify 6,000 scents has

  (a) an average sense of smell.

  (b) a below-average sense of smell.

  (c) an above-average sense of smell.

  (d) an extremely sensitive sense of smell.

5. When might someone not know they were eating a piece of apple?

  (a) when it was a cold day and the apple was not cooked

  (b) when they were eating quickly and the apple wasn't ripe

  (c) when they were blindfolded and an onion was held under their nose

  (d) when they had a sensitive sense of smell and a small apple piece

Name that Mammal!

These are new words to practice.
Say each word 10 times.

✳ fact	✳ vast
✳ fiction	✳ horde
✳ aggressive	✳ consume
✳ migration	✳ plague

**Before or after reading the story, write one sentence
that contains at least one new word.**

_____

_____

_____

_____

Name that Mammal!

Ms. Shin said, "Class, I want you to name a mammal. I will tell you facts about the animal. A fact is something that is true and not made-up. A fact is not fiction. Some of the facts I tell you may sound as if they are fiction, but they are not.

"This mammal is very aggressive. Aggressive animals are ready to quarrel or start fights. They are bold and active. The mammal migrated west from Asia. When something migrates, it moves to a new place to make a new home. There are eyewitness accounts from 1729. The accounts describe vast, or enormous, hordes of this animal. A horde is a large group or crowd.

"People describe seeing the animals swim across the mighty Volga River in Russia. When the hordes reached the far shore, they shook themselves off and made their way into houses and buildings. They couldn't swim across the Atlantic Ocean like they swam across the Volga River, but they did get to the Americas on sailing ships. They quickly advanced across the continents.

"Their vast numbers means huge amounts of food are consumed, or eaten. In fact, these mammals consume around one-fifth of the world's crops each year! In some Asian countries, they consume one-fourth! In the A.D. 1300s, one-third of the entire population of Europe died from the bubonic plague. The bubonic plague is also known as the Black Death. A plague is a deadly disease that spreads rapidly from person to person. How did these mammals spread the plague? These mammals had fleas. The fleas bit them. Then, when the fleas jumped to humans and bit the humans, the humans got the disease."

Ms. Shin said, "My last fact concerns the mammal's sharp front teeth. This mammal is constantly gnawing on hard objects, including pipes and electrical cables. This is because its front teeth never stop growing. It constantly gnaws to keep its teeth short and sharp." "Now," said Ms. Shin, "Name that mammal!" Ms. Shin was pleased when her students named the mammal. What mammal did the students name? They named the rat.

Name that Mammal!

After reading the story, answer the questions.
Fill in the circle next to the correct answer.

1. Around how much of the world's crops do rats consume each year?

   (a) 1/2
   (b) 1/3
   (c) 1/4
   (d) 1/5

2. From this story, you can tell that one way to prevent the spread of the bubonic plague, or Black Death, is to

   (a) wash your hands.
   (b) take pills and medicine.
   (c) not scratch your flea bites.
   (d) keep the number of rats down.

3. This story is mainly about

   (a) mammals.
   (b) facts about one mammal.
   (c) how a mammal was named.
   (d) a mammal and the Black Death.

4. What is *not* a reason that there are such vast hordes of rats?

   (a) they have large litters
   (b) they are strong swimmers
   (c) they have to stay in one place
   (d) they have many litters in a single year

5. Think about how the word *constant* relates to *once*. What two words relate in the same way?

constant : once

   (a) horde : crowd
   (b) fact : fiction
   (c) mammal : animal
   (d) vast : enormous

The Eiffel Tower, Meteorites, and Our Diet

These are new words to practice.

Say each word 10 times.

* meteor
* atmosphere
* meteorite
* matter

* hemoglobin
* oxygen
* compounds
* ores

Before or after reading the story, write one sentence that contains at least one new word.

_____

_____

_____

_____

The Eiffel Tower, Meteorites, and Our Diet

The Eiffel Tower is a huge tower in France. It was built in 1889. It is 984 feet (300 m) high. A meteor is commonly called a shooting star. A meteor is a solid body that moves with great speed from outer space into Earth's atmosphere. When it hits Earth's atmosphere, it is made white-hot by friction. It usually burns up. If the meteor does not burn up completely, the part that reaches the ground is called a meteorite. What do the Eiffel Tower and meteorites have in common with our diet?

All three share an element. An element is the building block of matter. Everything in the universe is made up of matter. Elements have only one type of atom. The element the Eiffel Tower, meteorites, and our diet have in common is iron.

Eiffel Tower

Iron is a metal. The symbol for iron is Fe. The symbol comes from the old Latin word *ferrum*. *Ferrum* means iron. In order to keep our bodies healthy, we need a small amount of iron in our diet. Spinach, red meat, fish, and egg yolks are all iron-rich foods.

We need iron because it is part of a substance in red blood cells called hemoglobin. As blood passes through the lungs, oxygen attaches itself to the iron in the hemoglobin. This turns the blood a bright red color. As the blood passes through the body, it delivers oxygen to every cell in the body. As the oxygen is used up, the blood changes to a purplish color.

Meteorites contain iron. Long ago, people used meteorites to make iron tools. Very few meteorites reach Earth, so iron tools were rare. Then, about 3,000 years ago, people learned how to use iron in the Earth's crust. Iron in the Earth's crust is a compound. A compound is a substance made of two or more elements. Iron compounds are called ores. People learned how to heat up the ores and separate the iron. This marked the start of the Iron Age. The Eiffel Tower is made of iron, as are many other things today.

The Eiffel Tower, Meteorites, and Our Diet

After reading the story, answer the questions.
Fill in the circle next to the correct answer.

1. If you see a shooting star, you are seeing

   (a) a meteorite in outer space.

   (b) a star moving with great speed.

   (c) a meteor hitting Earth's atmosphere.

   (d) a compound made white-hot by friction.

2. This story is mainly about

   (a) an element.

   (b) meteorites.

   (c) hemoglobin.

   (d) iron compounds.

3. When blood is a purplish color,

   (a) it has little iron.

   (b) it has little cells.

   (c) it has little oxygen.

   (d) it has little hemoglobin.

4. Think about how the word *crust* relates to *atmosphere*. What two words relate in the same way?

   > **crust : atmosphere**

   (a) water : lake

   (b) ground : air

   (c) grass : plant

   (d) mountain : valley

5. What is the symbol for iron?

   (a) Fe

   (b) Fn

   (c) Fo

   (d) Fr

Out-of-Control Twitching

These are new words to practice.

Say each word 10 times.

✳ twitched	✳ tic
✳ syndrome	✳ uncontrollable
✳ neurological	✳ vocal
✳ symptom	✳ interviewed

**Before or after reading the story, write one sentence
that contains at least one new word.**

_____

_____

_____

Out-of-Control Twitching

When one reads, one needs to keep ones eyes focused on the lines. But what if one twitched without warning? What if one's arms, legs, or neck twitched so violently that one lost one's place every few seconds?

Tourette syndrome is a neurological disorder. If something is neurological, it has to do with our nerves. Neurology is the study of the nervous system. Neurologists study our nervous system. Neurologists are still learning about Tourette syndrome. A syndrome is a group of signs and symptoms that occur together. People with Tourette syndrome have certain behaviors and show many of the same symptoms. What behaviors do people with Tourette syndrome show? They have tics.

A tic is a twitch of a muscle that cannot be controlled. People with Tourette syndrome have uncontrollable muscular and vocal tics. A vocal tic is spoken. It may be a word or a loud sound. People with Tourette syndrome cannot control how loud the sounds are or when they come out.

Brad Cohen has Tourette syndrome. When he was little, people did not know what was wrong with him. Brad would "woop" several times a minute, or he would make a series of loud "wah, wah, wah" sounds. People thought Brad was making the noises on purpose. They thought he just wanted to get attention and disrupt the class. Brad would also twitch uncontrollably. His tics made it very difficult for Brad to learn how to read. People made fun of him, and he did not have friends. He was told to leave restaurants and other public places.

Brad Cohen

Brad never gave up his dream of being a teacher, despite what people thought about him and the way he was treated. Brad interviewed for teaching jobs. When one is interviewed, one meets with someone. Brad was turned down 24 times before he was finally hired. Brad explained to his students and their parents that his uncontrollable tics were part of him. Brad showed that he could be an excellent teacher. One reason Brad was such a good teacher was that he knew firsthand how hard one has to work to learn.

94

Out-of-Control Twitching

After reading the story, answer the questions.
Fill in the circle next to the correct answer.

1. This story is mainly about

(a) learning how to read.

(b) what muscular and vocal tics are.

(c) a man with a neurological disorder.

(d) how hard it was for one man to be a teacher.

2. A neurologist would most likely study

(a) the flu and how it is spread.

(b) why our bones break and how they mend.

(c) our hearts and how to keep them strong.

(d) how our brain sends messages to our legs to move.

3. How many times did Brad interview before he was hired?

(a) 24

(b) 25

(c) 26

(d) 27

4. Think about how the word *twitching* relates to *still*. What words relate in the same way?

> **twitching : still**

(a) hard : difficult

(b) unspoken : vocal

(c) seconds : minutes

(d) tic : uncontrollable

5. From the story, you can tell that

(a) people know a lot about Tourette syndrome.

(b) Brad does not like eating in restaurants.

(c) all tics are a sign of Tourette syndrome.

(d) sometimes people cannot help the way they behave.

Pus — A Sign of Battle

These are new words to practice.
Say each word 10 times.

* pus   * cells

* circulatory   * engulf

* powerful   * antibodies

* blood vessels   * invaders

**Before or after reading the story, write one sentence
that contains at least one new word.**

_____

_____

_____

_____

Pus — A Sign of Battle

Pus is a thick, yellowish or whitish matter. It oozes from infected sores or cuts. Pus may look gross, but it is actually a sign of battle. It is a sign that our body is working to protect itself. How can this be?

Our circulatory system is made up of our heart, blood, and blood vessels. Our heart is a powerful muscle about the size of one's fist. It is in the middle of one's chest, tilted slightly to the left. The heart is a powerful pump. It pushes blood around one's body through tubes called blood vessels. Every person has about 60,000 miles (96,000 km) of blood vessels in their body's circulatory system!

Our bodies are made up of different types of cells. Blood carries oxygen and food to all of the cells in our body. Blood carries waste away from the cells. Blood also helps to protect the cells. Blood is made up of red cells, white cells, platelets, and plasma. There are different types of white blood cells, but all white blood cells have the same job: they all help our body fight disease and infection.

1. Some white blood cells attack germs, or bacteria. The white blood cells find the bacteria by the chemicals the germs release. Then, when a white blood cell finds the germ, it starts to engulf it. When something is engulfed, it is covered completely. It is swallowed up. Bacteria can enter a body through an open sore or cut. Why is pus found at this location? Pus is mostly made up of dead white blood cells. Pus is a sign that white blood cells found and battled germs.

2. Other white blood cells produce, or make, chemicals. They produce chemicals called antibodies. Antibodies are chemicals that help our body fight against infection. Other types of white blood cells move freely around the body. They attack and engulf tiny invaders. The tiny invaders cannot be seen without a microscope. The invaders include bacteria, viruses, and pieces of old, dead cells.

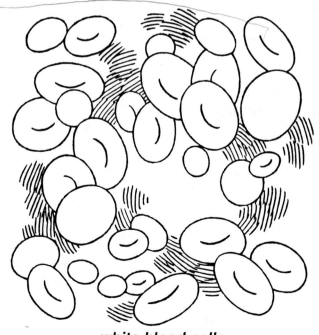

white blood cells

Pus — A Sign of Battle

After reading the story, answer the questions.
Fill in the circle next to the correct answer.

1. How many different types of white blood cells were mentioned in the story?

   (a) one
   (b) two
   (c) three
   (d) four

2. What is not listed as making up part of our blood?

   (a) plasma
   (b) oxygen
   (c) platelets
   (d) red blood cells

3. This story is mainly about

   (a) battles.
   (b) our hearts.
   (c) blood vessels.
   (d) white blood cells.

4. From the story, you can tell that an invader is

   (a) a type of white blood cell.
   (b) a chemical that is released.
   (c) a thing that enters or breaks in.
   (d) an antibody that helps fight infection.

5. Think about how the word *tiny* relates to *small*. What two words relate in the same way?

   | tiny : small |

   (a) red : white
   (b) open : covered
   (c) different : same
   (d) powerful : strong

An Inventor
Who Was Paid Less

These are new words to practice.
Say each word 10 times.

* guarantee   * technical

* issued   * patent

* submit   * descriptions

* application   * filament

**Before or after reading the story, write one sentence
that contains at least one new word.**

_____

_____

_____

_____

An Inventor
Who Was Paid Less

Lewis Latimer was just an office boy. He worked in an office that helped people prepare patents. A patent is a guarantee from the government to an inventor. It guarantees that the inventor is the only one who may allow that product to be made or sold. To be issued a patent, an inventor has to submit, or send in, an application. The application was very complicated. It had many forms. Technical drawings had to be submitted, too.

Lewis Latimer

Latimer had very little schooling, but he wanted to be more than just an office boy. He watched the drafters in the office. The drafters were the men who drew the technical drawings. The drawings showed how the inventions fit together. The drawings were accompanied with detailed descriptions. The descriptions told how the invention worked.

On his own, Latimer bought used drafting tools. He could not afford new ones. He bought books. One day he asked if he could make some drawings. He was laughed at. Finally, he was told he could try one drawing. Latimer's skill astonished everyone. Latimer was given a job as a draftsman. Then he was moved up to head draftsman. Despite his position, Latimer was paid less than every other draftsman.

Latimer was paid less because of the color of his skin. Latimer was a black man. His parents had been slaves. Over the years, Latimer made great contributions to science. Alexander Graham Bell invented the telephone. Bell had to race to submit his patent application because other inventors were submitting similar ones. Latimer drew Bell's drawings and wrote the descriptions for his patent. Bell was issued his patent thanks to Latimer's fast, hard work.

Latimer worked with Thomas Alva Edison for many years. Edison invented many things, but so did Latimer. One of Latimer's inventions led to cheap light bulbs. The invention was a new way of building filaments. Filaments are thin, threadlike conductors of electricity inside light bulbs. When an electric current passes through it, the filament lights up.

An Inventor
Who Was Paid Less

After reading the story, answer the questions.
Fill in the circle next to the correct answer.

1. How many inventors were mentioned by name in the story besides Latimer?

(a) one

(b) two

(c) three

(d) four

2. This story is mainly about

(a) patents.

(b) Latimer learning how to draw.

(c) a hard-working inventor.

(d) how Bell got his telephone patent.

3. What below is most likely a technical drawing?

(a) a drawing of your room

(b) a drawing of the sunset

(c) a drawing of a car motor

(d) a drawing of two cats playing

4. Think about how the word *draftsman* relates to *draws*. What two words relate in the same way?

draftsman : draws

(a) doctor : heals

(b) musician : drum

(c) dentist : teeth

(d) builder : house

5. From the story, you can tell that

(a) people should not be paid the same.

(b) patent applications are easier today.

(c) Latimer was afraid of people laughing at him.

(d) being smart has nothing to do with skin color.

A Huge Area
in a Small Space

These are new words to practice.

Say each word 10 times.

* internal   * lining

* digestive tract   * projection

* esophagus   * villi

* intestine   * microvilli

Before or after reading the story, write one sentence
that contains at least one new word.

_____

_____

_____

_____

A Huge Area in a Small Space

You have a very large internal part. When something is internal, it is inside. It is part of something. This internal part is about 2,700 square feet (250 square meters). It covers an area 10 times greater than the area your skin covers. It can almost cover a basketball court! But this internal part fits inside a 20-foot tube! How could something with such a huge surface area fit into such a small space? What in the world could this internal part be?

Your gut or digestive tract is where our food is digested. Digestion is how we change the food we eat into the energy and nutrients our body needs. Our digestive tract is made of several parts that the food travels through. It takes about 20 to 40 hours for food to travel through the digestive tract.

Our digestive tract begins in the mouth. From the mouth, it goes to the esophagus. The esophagus is a tube that runs from our mouth down our throat to our stomach. From the stomach, food passes into the small intestine. Despite its name, the small intestine is the biggest part of our digestive system! The small intestine is a tube about 20 feet (6 m) long. It is about 1.5 inches (3.8 cm) thick. It is all folded up. It fits below our rib cage.

Our internal part that is large enough to almost cover a basketball court is the inner wall or lining of the small intestine. The lining is folded and ridged. It is also covered in millions of tiny projections. A projection is something that projects, or sticks out. The finger-like projections on the lining wall are called villi. The tiny villi are covered in even tinier projections called microvilli.

The folds, villi, and microvilli make the inner surface area of the small intestine much bigger than it would be if it were just a smooth tube. The folds and projections make it about 600 times bigger! Nutrients from digested food pass into our blood. They pass through the villi into the blood.

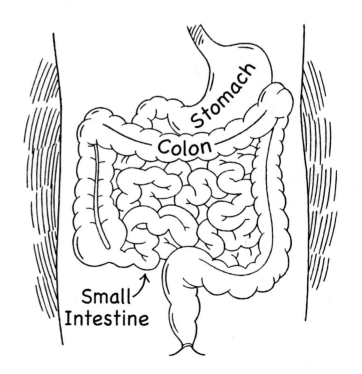

A Huge Area in a Small Space

After reading the story, answer the questions.
Fill in the circle next to the correct answer.

1. This story is mainly about

   ⓐ why we digest food.

   ⓑ millions of tiny projections.

   ⓒ the lining of our small intestine.

   ⓓ how parts of our digestive system work.

2. What is the correct sequence for how food passes through the digestive tract?

   ⓐ mouth, stomach, small intestine, esophagus

   ⓑ mouth, stomach, esophagus, small intestine

   ⓒ mouth, esophagus, stomach, small intestine

   ⓓ mouth, esophagus, small intestine, stomach

3. Which answer below is not a reason the lining of the small intestine have such a large surface area?

   ⓐ it has folds

   ⓑ it is internal

   ⓒ it has projections

   ⓓ it is covered in villi

4. Why would the author say that the lining of the small intestine could almost cover a basketball court?

   ⓐ it helps the reader understand our gut

   ⓑ it helps the reader understand how big it is

   ⓒ it helps the reader understand how it is internal

   ⓓ it helps the reader understand how digestion works

5. Think about how the word *villi* relates to *microvilli*. What two words relate in the same way?

   | villi : microvilli |

   ⓐ sky : blue

   ⓑ foot : hands

   ⓒ wheels : circle

   ⓓ trunk : branches

The Changing Planet Number

These are new words to practice.

Say each word 10 times.

✻ solar system	✻ astronomer
✻ generation	✻ doubt
✻ oval	✻ gravity
✻ distant	✻ vote

**Before or after reading the story, write one sentence
that contains at least one new word.**

_____

_____

_____

_____

The Changing Planet Number

Ty studied our solar system in school. He learned that the sun is the center of our solar system. He learned that planets orbit the sun. They go around it. There are eight planets. Ty's father, grandfather, and great-grandfather learned about our solar system in school, too. All four generations learned about the solar system. But each generation did not learn the same thing!

Ty and his great-grandfather learned that the solar system has eight planets. Ty's father and grandfather learned that the solar system had nine planets. Are there eight or nine planets? What generations were taught the correct number of planets?

Pluto was discovered on February 18, 1930. Pluto's orbit is shaped like an oval. The oval-shaped orbit means that sometimes Pluto is closer to the sun than at other times. The closeness depends on where Pluto is in its orbit. It takes 248 years for Pluto to complete its orbit around the sun. For most of its orbit, Pluto is farther away from the sun than any other planet. However, for 20 years of its orbit, Pluto is not the most distant. During those years, the planet Neptune is the most distant.

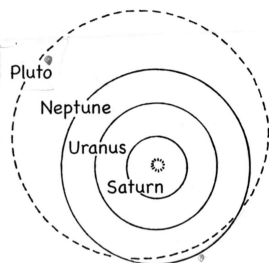

the orbits of the outer planets

Some astronomers began to doubt, or question, if Pluto really was a planet. Astronomers are scientists who study stars and planets. They study space. Why did the astronomers have doubts? Pluto was the smallest planet by far. Earth's moon is bigger than Pluto. Gravity is a force. It is a force of attraction. Pluto's gravitational force is very small when compared to bigger planets.

Pluto was called a planet for 76 years. In August 2006, a vote was taken by astronomers. The outcome of the vote was that Pluto was no longer a planet. Ty learned about the solar system after August 2006. Ty's great-grandfather learned about the planets before Pluto's discovery in 1930. At those times, there were only eight planets. Ty's father and grandfather went to school at different times. They went after Pluto's discovery. They went before astronomers decided it was not a planet.

The Changing Planet Number

After reading the story, answer the questions.
Fill in the circle next to the correct answer.

1. This story is mainly about

  (a) Pluto.

  (b) a vote.

  (c) gravity.

  (d) what Ty learned.

2. Ty's great-grandfather was taught that there were eight planets because

  (a) he went to school after 1930.

  (b) Pluto had not yet been discovered.

  (c) the vote outcome was that Pluto was no longer a planet.

  (d) Pluto's gravitation force is less than the other planets.

3. Which answer lists three generations?

  (a) a girl and her two sisters

  (b) a girl, her sister, and her mother

  (c) a girl, her mother, and her grandmother

  (d) a girl, her mother, her grandmother, and her great grandmother

4. From the story, one can tell that what is learned in school

  (a) will be voted on.

  (b) is always the same.

  (c) was not correct long ago.

  (d) may change as new things are discovered.

5. Think about how the word *doubt* relates to *question*. What two words relate in the same way?

  doubt : question

  (a) discover : find

  (b) complete : start

  (d) force : attraction

  (d) decide : astronomer

Why a Termite Eats Its Skin

These are new words to practice.
Say each word 10 times.

* armor   * cellulose

* contain   * protozoa

* cell   * nourishment

* nutrients   * consume

Before or after reading the story, write one sentence that contains at least one new word.

_____

_____

_____

_____

Why a Termite Eats Its Skin

A termite is an insect. All insects have skin that is like armor. Armor is a hard, protective coat. The armor-like skin may protect the termite, but it does not allow it room to grow. For this reason, the termite sheds, or loses, its tough skin several times during its life. After a termite has finished shedding its old skin, the termite immediately eats it. Why would a termite eat tough, old, armor-like skin?

Termites eat wood. Wood is made up of cells that contain nutrients a termite needs. A cell is the basic unit of living matter. All plants and animals are made up of one or more cells. Wood cells contain fats and proteins. They contain vitamins and minerals. To get the nutrients from the wood cells, a termite first has to break down the cell walls. Wood cell walls are mainly made up of cellulose. Termites cannot break down, or digest, the cellulose. They need help.

termite

Help comes in the form of tiny, one-celled protozoa. Protozoa are very tiny, animal-like creatures. The protozoa live and swim inside a termite's intestines. When the termite eats wood, the tiny creatures break down the cellulose found in the walls of the wood cells. They break the cellulose down into sugars. The sugars are in a form that the termites can use for nourishment.

When a termite sheds its skin, it loses all of the tiny protozoa living and swimming in its intestines. This is because when a termite loses its skin, it also loses the inside lining of its digestive system. The entire inside lining is lost, from the mouth to the intestines.

When the termite immediately consumes, or eats, its own skin, it is also consuming the one-celled creatures before they die. By consuming the skin, the termite reintroduces the protozoa back into its intestines. With the protozoa in its intestines, the termite can continue to gain nourishment. The termite can get fats and proteins. It can get vitamins and minerals. It can continue to grow because it can get all the nourishment it needs.

Why a Termite Eats Its Skin

After reading the story, answer the questions.
Fill in the circle next to the correct answer.

1. What would happen if a termite did not eat the skin it shed?

    (a) the termite would grow a new armor-like skin

    (b) the termite would not be able to digest cellulose

    (c) the termite would lose the lining of its intestines

    (d) the termite would need more wood for extra nourishment

2. This story is mainly about

    (a) termites and cells.

    (b) the life of termites.

    (c) insects with armor-like skin.

    (d) termites and how they get nourishment.

3. The tiny animal-like creatures in a termite's intestines are made up of how many cells?

    (a) one

    (b) two

    (c) three

    (d) four

4. Think about how the word *shed* relates to *lose*. What two words relate in the same way?

> **shed : lose**

    (a) finish : go

    (b) digest : gain

    (c) consume : eat

    (d) continue : end

5. What do the protozoa break down the cellulose into?

    (a) fats

    (b) sugars

    (c) vitamins

    (d) proteins

Making Bread Taste Sweet

These are new words to practice.

Say each word 10 times.

- ✷ nutrients
- ✷ carbohydrates
- ✷ protein
- ✷ digestive tract

- ✷ saliva
- ✷ enzyme
- ✷ starch
- ✷ glucose

**Before or after reading the story, write one sentence
that contains at least one new word.**

_____

_____

_____

_____

Making Bread Taste Sweet

Suzu chewed on a piece of bread. Instead of swallowing the bread, Suzu let the chewed bread stay in her mouth. After a few minutes, the bread began to taste sweet. Marshall chewed on a piece of cheese. Instead of swallowing the cheese, Marshall let the chewed cheese stay in his mouth. The cheese in Marshall's mouth did not begin to taste sweet.

Why did chewed bread begin to taste sweet? Why didn't chewed cheese begin to taste sweet? We digest our food. Digestion is when we change the food we eat into the energy and nutrients our body needs. The main nutrients in food are carbohydrates, fats, and proteins. Vitamins and minerals are also important nutrients. We digest our food in our digestive tract. Our digestive tract is made of several parts. Our digestive tract begins in the mouth.

When we chew our food, we crush it and mash it. Chewing our food also mixes it with salvia, or spit. The saliva comes from three pairs of salivary glands. One pair of salivary glands is at the back of the mouth. One pair is under the tongue. One pair is under the sides of the lower jaw. Our salivary glands begin to produce saliva when we smell or chew our food.

The saliva we produce has a special enzyme. An enzyme is a protein. The enzyme in our saliva helps to break down food into the nutrients that the body can use. It helps to change starch into sugar. Starches are carbohydrates stored in plants. Bread, pasta, potatoes, and rice are all starchy foods rich in carbohydrates.

Remember that Suzu chewed bread, and the bread in her mouth began to taste sweet. Bread is high in carbohydrates. The enzyme in Suzu's saliva began to change the bread into glucose. Glucose is a form of sugar that the body uses for energy. Suzu could taste the glucose. Marshall chewed a piece of cheese. Cheese is high in protein, but it is not a starchy food. The cheese did not begin to taste sweet because it was not high in carbohydrates.

Making Bread Taste Sweet

**After reading the story, answer the questions.
Fill in the circle next to the correct answer.**

1. What helps to change carbohydrates to glucose?

   ⓐ a sugar
   ⓑ a starch
   ⓒ a protein
   ⓓ an enzyme

2. What chewed food would be the least likely to begin to taste sweet if you kept it in your mouth for a few minutes?

   ⓐ noodles
   ⓑ chicken
   ⓒ crackers
   ⓓ French fries

3. This story is mainly about

   ⓐ an enzyme.
   ⓑ what makes some foods starchy.
   ⓒ how all of our digestive tract works.
   ⓓ why some chewed foods begin to taste sweet.

4. Why might it be important to eat different kinds of foods?

   ⓐ Starchy foods are high in carbohydrates.
   ⓑ Our salivary glands need to produce enzymes.
   ⓒ Different foods have different nutrients.
   ⓓ Minerals and vitamins are high-protein foods.

5. Think about how the word *produce* relates to *make*. What two words relate in the same way?

produce : make

   ⓐ grow : rice
   ⓑ crush : mash
   ⓒ help : digest
   ⓓ start : finish

Donya's Guides

These are new words to practice.
Say each word 10 times.

* burrow	* inhabitant
* immense	* pygmies
* chimpanzee	* nomadic
* original	* penetrate

Before or after reading the story, write one sentence that contains at least one new word.

_____

_____

_____

_____

Donya's Guides

Donya was told that it wouldn't be wise to sit directly on the ground. When she asked why, she was told, "See how the ground is covered with leaf litter? Worms that can burrow, or dig a hole, into your skin live in the leaf litter. The worms will burrow through your clothes and into you." Where in the world was Donya?

Donya was in a lowland tropical forest. The forest was immense, or very large. The immense forest stretched across the Congo Basin in Central Africa. Donya had come to study chimpanzees. She was going to live in the tropical forest, or jungle, for four years. During that time, she was going to look for chimpanzees. She wanted to find out what they ate, how they survived, and how they behaved socially.

Donya found quickly that she needed help. She had to hire guides. The guides were the original forest inhabitants. An original inhabitant is the first person to live in a certain area or place. Who were the original inhabitants? The original inhabitants were the Biaka people. The Biaka people were pygmies. Despite being shorter than most people, the Biaka pygmies were experts in jungle survival.

Hunters and gatherers, the Biaka originally lived a nomadic lifestyle. When one is nomadic, one does not stay in one place. One wanders from place to place. The Biaka wandered through the vast jungle looking for food. They ate bats, caterpillars, and termites. They ate what scarce fruits and nuts they could find. Sometimes they would try to scare animals into nets. They could quickly build a hut made with bent branches and covered in huge leaves for shelter.

Donya felt that the jungle seemed like a place of constant twilight. This was because it was rare for sunlight to penetrate, or get through, the thick forest layers. She wrote that she would not have been able to survive without her guides, as her guides kept her from getting lost in the place where light rarely penetrated—and from burrowing worms!

Donya's Guides

**After reading the story, answer the questions.
Fill in the circle next to the correct answer.**

1. The story does not say that the Biaka

   a) are experts in jungle survival.

   b) are taller than most other people.

   c) originally lived a nomadic lifestyle.

   d) ate bats, caterpillars, and termites.

2. From the story, you can tell that

   a) most scientists study something for four years.

   b) lots of scientists have gone to the Congo Basin.

   c) scientists sometimes need the knowledge of original inhabitants.

   d) today scientists study chimpanzees in places where it is not as easy to get lost.

3. This story is mainly about

   a) burrowing worms.

   b) how pygmies survive.

   c) where chimpanzees live.

   d) Donya and who helped her.

4. Why did Donya feel that the jungle was like a place of constant twilight?

   a) The jungle was gloomy.

   b) It was easy to get lost.

   c) She lived there for four years.

   d) There was leaf litter on the ground.

5. Think about how the word *immense* relates to *small*. What two words relate in the same way?

   immense : small

   a) dark : light

   b) gloomy : dim

   c) original : new

   d) inhabitant : chimpanzee

The Last Pigeon

These are new words to practice.
Say each word 10 times.

✳ pigeon	✳ flocks
✳ native	✳ infinite
✳ species	✳ extinct
✳ migratory	✳ slaughter

Before or after reading the story, write one sentence
that contains at least one new word.

_____

_____

_____

_____

The Last Pigeon

There were billions of passenger pigeons. Passenger pigeons were a native species of North America. A native species is a kind of animal or plant that was born or belongs naturally in a certain place or country. A native species is not introduced. Passenger pigeons were once the most common bird in North America. Some scientists think it was quite possibly the most common bird on Earth.

Passenger pigeons were migratory. When something is migratory, it does not stay in one place. The pigeons migrated northward and southward across the continent. They migrated in large flocks, or groups. How large were the flocks? Some flocks contained more than 100 million birds! When these large flocks of birds flew overhead, they would darken the sky! Their flapping wings sounded like the roar of distant thunder.

passenger pigeon

One early explorer said there was "an infinite number." Something infinite has no limits. It is very great or vast. There are no passenger pigeons alive today. The bird is extinct. When something is extinct, it is no longer alive. There is no more of its species living. How could the passenger pigeon become extinct if it seemed that there was an infinite number?

Passenger pigeons were good to eat. They were easy to kill. Settlers from Europe brought guns. The birds had no defense against this modern weapon. The railroad also was a factor in the birds' extinction. The railroads made it possible for the dead birds to be shipped. They could be shipped to cities far away. There, people could feast on the delicious meat.

Hunters would wait in the birds' nesting grounds. When the birds settled, they would start the slaughter. It was easy for hunting parties to slaughter 50,000 birds in a week. A hunter shot the last passenger pigeon ever seen in the wild on March 24, 1900. The passenger pigeon became extinct on September 1, 1914. That was the day the last bird died. The bird died in the Cincinnati Zoo.

The Last Pigeon

**After reading the story, answer the questions.
Fill in the circle next to the correct answer.**

1. Which phrase best completes this sentence: "The night sky was lit by _____ number of twinkling stars."

   (a) a species

   (b) a slaughter

   (c) a migratory

   (d) an infinite

2. This story is mainly about

   (a) how pigeons are good to eat.

   (b) how a species became extinct.

   (c) how the passenger pigeon was hunted.

   (d) how many passenger pigeons there were.

3. Which answer shows 100 million and 100 billion, in that order?

   (a) 1,000,000; 1,000,000,000

   (b) 100,000,000; 100,000,000,000

   (c) 100,000,000,000; 100,000,000

   (d) 100,000,000; 100,000,000,000,000

4. Think about how the word *bird* relates to *flock*. What two words relate in the same way?

   | bird : flock |

   (a) dog : pack

   (b) cow : cows

   (c) deer : buck

   (d) goose : geese

5. Why didn't the passenger pigeon become extinct when the hunter shot the last bird ever seen in the wild?

   (a) there were a few passenger pigeons in some zoos

   (b) there was an infinite number of passenger pigeons

   (c) railroads no longer could be used to ship the birds

   (d) a few passenger pigeons had migrated to cities far away

A Doctor Who Listened with Fingertips

These are new words to practice.

Say each word 10 times.

* dyslexia
* distorted
* reversed
* struggle

* cardiology
* pediatric
* stethoscope
* shunt

Before or after reading the story, write one sentence that contains at least one new word.

_____

_____

_____

_____

120

A Doctor Who Listened with Fingertips

Helen Brooke Taussig stared at the word. Was it "was" or "saw"? Helen could not tell because the word seemed to change as she looked at it. Today, we know that Helen suffered from dyslexia. Dyslexia is a condition in which letters and words appear distorted or reversed on the page. When something is distorted, it is twisted out of its usual shape or look. When something is reversed, it is backward.

Helen was a very slow reader because of her dyslexia. Helen was very bright. It was only reading that was a struggle. Every day, Helen spent extra hours reading, making sure that she learned everything. Helen went on to college and medical school. She struggled with her dyslexia the entire time.

Dr. Helen Brooke Taussig

Helen studied cardiology. A cardiologist studies the heart. Helen was a pediatric cardiologist. Pediatrics is a branch of medicine that has to do with the care and treatment of babies and children. A pediatric cardiologist is a heart doctor for children. A terrible thing happened just when Helen was about to begin her duties in 1930. Helen began to lose her hearing.

Doctors use a stethoscope to listen to a patient's heartbeat, or pulse. Unable to hear, Helen could not use a stethoscope. Once again, Helen did not give up. She figured out a new way to listen to a child's heart. She used her hands! She would rest her fingertips on a child's chest. She would apply gentle pressure. She would "listen" with her fingertips. She could tell if something was wrong by feeling the pulse's rhythm, or beat.

At that time, many "blue babies" died. "Blue babies" were babies that were not getting enough oxygen. The lack of oxygen caused their skin to appear bluish. Helen figured out a way to help. She wanted to build a shunt. A shunt is a passageway. The shunt would allow more blood to flow to a baby's lungs. Helen went to a famous surgeon. Together they found a way for her idea to work. Today, thanks to Helen's idea, many "blue babies" survive to adulthood.

A Doctor Who Listened with Fingertips

**After reading the story, answer the questions.
Fill in the circle next to the correct answer.**

1. This story is mainly about

   (a) what dyslexia is.

   (b) a doctor who struggled.

   (c) helping "blue babies" get oxygen.

   (d) how to listen without a stethoscope.

2. What did Helen do because of her dyslexia?

   (a) She became a pediatric cardiologist.

   (b) She figured out a way to build a shunt.

   (c) She spent extra hours reading every day.

   (d) She learned to listen with her fingertips.

3. The mirror made everyone look tall and funny. The mirror _____ everyone's shape.

   (a) reversed

   (b) distorted

   (c) reflected

   (d) struggled

4. What did Helen's shunt do?

   (a) let in more oxygen

   (b) put gentle pressure on a baby's heart

   (c) explain why a baby's skin was bluish

   (d) allow more blood to flow to a baby's lungs

5. Think about how the word *hear* relates to *stethoscope*. What two words relate in the same way?

hear : stethoscope

   (a) wear : pants

   (b) mouth : taste

   (c) see : glasses

   (d) scissors : cut

The Wrong Door

These are new words to practice.
Say each word 10 times.

* contestant   * odds

* participating   * probability

* host   * offers

* assure   * exchange

Before or after reading the story, write one sentence
that contains at least one new word.

_____

_____

_____

_____

The Wrong Door

You have been picked to be a contestant. A contestant is a person who takes part in a contest. You are participating, or taking part, in a game show. You are participating in a contest where the prize is one million dollars. Your host, or the person who has invited you as a guest on the show, shows you three identical doors. It is guaranteed, or assured, that the prize is behind one of the three identical doors.

You are very happy to be a participant, and you choose one of the doors. How assured are you of success? You cannot be assured of success, but you can figure out your odds, or chances. The probability, or likelihood, of your being correct is one in three. The odds of you having chosen the correct door are one in three. You inform your host of your decision, but then something happens.

Your host opens up one of the other two doors. You are happy to see that the prize is not behind the opened door. You still have a chance to win the million dollars. Your host offers, or puts forward, a possible exchange. An exchange is when one thing is traded for another. You can exchange your door for the other unopened door. Should you switch? Should you take your host up on his exchange offer?

Most contestants do not. This is because they think the chances of both unopened doors being correct are the same. They think the probability is even. The truth is that one has a better chance of winning the million dollars if one switches doors! How can this be?

If you switched, the only way you could lose was to have picked the door with the prize behind it at the beginning. But remember that with your first choice, the probability of being correct was one in three. This meant that the probability that you were wrong was greater. The odds of being wrong were two in three. If you exchange doors, you are betting that your first guess was wrong—which it probably was!

The Wrong Door

After reading the story, answer the questions.
Fill in the circle next to the correct answer.

1. This story is mainly about

- ⓐ a host and an open door.
- ⓑ a one-million-dollar prize.
- ⓒ a game show and probability.
- ⓓ a contestant and a participant.

2. From the story, you can tell that

- ⓐ sometimes you increase your chance of winning by changing your answer.
- ⓑ you can never increase your chance of winning by changing your answer.
- ⓒ you can never win in a game where you can change your answer more than once.
- ⓓ your chance of winning always stays the same no matter what answer you choose.

3. Tanya _____ the smaller bike for a bigger one.

- ⓐ assured
- ⓑ exchanged
- ⓒ guaranteed
- ⓓ participated

4. When you toss a coin in the air, the probability of it coming down heads is

- ⓐ less than the probability of it landing on tails.
- ⓑ the same as the probability of it landing on tails.
- ⓒ greater than the probability of it landing on tails.
- ⓓ two in three the probability of it landing on tails.

5. Think about how the word *contestant* relates to *contest*. What two words relate in the same way?

contestant : contest

- ⓐ racer : race
- ⓑ biker : bike
- ⓒ swimmer : swim
- ⓓ driver : drive

The Tall-Man Solution

These are new words to practice.
Say each word 10 times.

* veterinarian

* solution

* aquarium

* nibbled

* lodged

* inserted

* contracted

* novel

Before or after reading the story, write one sentence
that contains at least one new word.

126

The Tall-Man Solution

The veterinarians had a life-and-death case. A veterinarian is a medical doctor for animals. The veterinarians' life-and-death case did not have an easy solution, or answer. Two dolphins had fallen ill. The dolphins were in an aquarium. An aquarium is a building or place. It is where collections of water animals and plants are shown to the public.

The dolphins had nibbled, or taken small bites, of plastic. The plastic they nibbled was from the edge of their pool. The plastic became lodged, or stuck, in the dolphins' stomachs. The plastic had made the dolphins very ill. It needed to be removed fast. How could the plastic be removed? The solution the doctors first came up was the usual one. Surgical instruments would be used. The tools would be inserted through the mouth. The tools would be long. They would reach down into the stomach.

This answer did not work. It failed. The dolphins' stomachs had contracted when the surgical instruments were inserted. When something contracts, it becomes smaller. It draws together. If the doctors had forced the instruments down into the contracted stomachs, they would have harmed the animals. There had to be a different solution.

The solution the veterinarians came up was novel. Something novel is new and different. The world's tallest living man was part of the solution. Bao Xishun, the world's tallest living man, was 7 feet, 9 inches tall. His arms were 41.7 inches (1.06 m) long. He was a herdsman from Inner Mongolia.

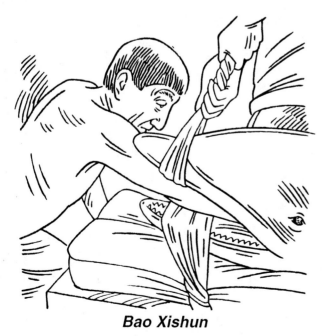

Bao Xishun

Xishun went to the aquarium. He carefully inserted his long arms into the dolphins' mouths. The dolphins could not bite Xishun because towels wrapped around the dolphins' jaws were holding them open. Other people's arms were not long enough to reach the plastic lodged in the dolphins' stomachs, but Xishun's were. The world's tallest living man was able to reach and grab the plastic pieces. Xishun was able to save the dolphins.

The Tall-Man Solution

After reading the story, answer the questions.
Fill in the circle next to the correct answer.

1. This story is mainly about

   ⓐ nibbling on plastic.

   ⓑ dolphins and aquariums.

   ⓒ the world's tallest living man.

   ⓓ a solution to a life-and-death problem.

2. Where was Bao Xishun from?

   ⓐ Mali

   ⓑ Montana

   ⓒ Mongolia

   ⓓ Mississippi

3. Why didn't veterinarians insert their own arms into the dolphins' stomachs?

   ⓐ They had surgical instruments.

   ⓑ Their arms were not long enough.

   ⓒ The dolphins' stomachs contracted.

   ⓓ They would have harmed the animals.

4. From the story, one can tell that

   ⓐ at some time Xishun will become taller.

   ⓑ at no time has a man ever been taller than Xishun.

   ⓒ at one time Xishun was the tallest man in the world.

   ⓓ at some time there will be a man taller than Xishun.

5. Think about how the word *contract* relates to *expand*. What two words relate in the same way?

contract : expand	—*opp.*

   ⓐ *new* novel : old

   ⓑ lodged : stuck ✗

   ⓒ solution : answer

   ⓓ veterinarian : animal

The Cent with a Scent

These are new words to practice.
Say each word 10 times.

* clutched   * absorbent

* perspiration   * sulfur

* scent   * acids

* copper   * hydrogen sulfide

**Before or after reading the story, write one sentence
that contains at least one new word.**

_____

_____

_____

The Cent with a Scent

Lita wanted to make the basketball team. To get in shape, Lita ran everywhere. One hot day, Lita's mother sent Lita to the store to buy a newspaper. Lita ran both ways. On the way back, she clutched the newspaper in one hand and her change of one old penny tightly in the other. Lita began to perspire, or sweat, but still she did not lessen her pace. She simply clutched the newspaper and penny more tightly so they would not slip out of her sweaty hands.

When Lita, dripping with perspiration, arrived home, she opened up her hands and put the newspaper and penny on the table. Much to Lita's surprise, the penny stunk! It had a nasty odor. It smelled like rotten eggs! "Mom," Lita cried, "My penny has a stinky odor. My old cent has a scent!" Lita's penny did have a nasty scent. But when Lita had her older brother smell the penny later that evening, the penny did not smell. What was going on?

Pennies contain copper. Copper is a metal. It is a very absorbent metal. When something is absorbent it is able to absorb. It is able to soak up or take something in. Copper is such an absorbent metal that it is able to pick up sulfur from the air. Sulfur is a chemical element. The sulfur makes the penny dirty, but it also does something else. The sulfur is what gives the cent a scent!

Our perspiration contains acids. Acids are a type of compound. A compound is a substance that contains two or more elements. Acids contain the element hydrogen. The absorbed sulfur combines with the acids in our perspiration to make hydrogen sulfide.

Hydrogen sulfide has a particular odor. What does hydrogen sulfide smell like? Hydrogen sulfide smells like rotten eggs! Lita's penny stank because she had been clutching it tightly while perspiring. The penny had lost its rotten egg scent when Lita's older brother smelled it. This was because the penny had dried while on the table. It was no longer damp from Lita's perspiration.

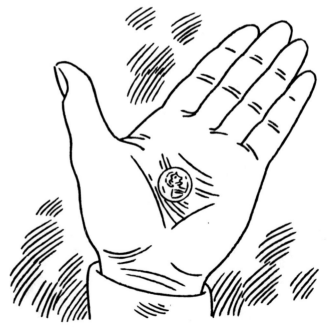

The Cent with a Scent

**After reading the story, answer the questions.
Fill in the circle next to the correct answer.**

1. This story is mainly about

   ⓐ when to clutch a penny.

   ⓑ why and when we perspire.

   ⓒ what smells like rotten eggs.

   ⓓ why and when a penny may stink.

2. Which statement is true?

   ⓐ Sulfur is an acid.

   ⓑ Sulfur is an element.

   ⓒ Sulfur is an absorbent metal.

   ⓓ Sulfur is a chemical compound.

3. Think about how the word *perspire* relates to *hot*. What two words relate in the same way?

perspire : hot

   ⓐ smile : sad

   ⓑ yawn : awake

   ⓒ shiver : cold

   ⓓ shake : brave

4. What information is not necessary to answer why a cent can have a scent?

   ⓐ Copper is an absorbent metal.

   ⓑ Our perspiration contains acids.

   ⓒ Lita wanted to make the basketball team.

   ⓓ Hydrogen sulfide smells like rotten eggs.

5. One reason dimes may not stink like pennies is that

   ⓐ dimes do not contain copper.

   ⓑ dimes are smaller than pennies.

   ⓒ dimes cannot absorb perspiration.

   ⓓ dimes are worth more than a cent.

Stopping Dizziness

These are new words to practice.
Say each word 10 times.

* twirling	* canal
* rapidly	* triggered
* prevent	* signals
* semicircular	* balance

Before or after reading the story, write one sentence that contains at least one new word.

_____

_____

_____

_____

Stopping Dizziness

Maggie was learning how to be an ice skater. She was practicing twirling on the ice. She spun, turning around rapidly. All the fast spinning began to make Maggie feel dizzy. Maggie stopped twirling, but she still felt as if the world were turning. Why would Maggie still feel dizzy once she had stopped twirling? How could she prevent, or stop, her feelings of dizziness?

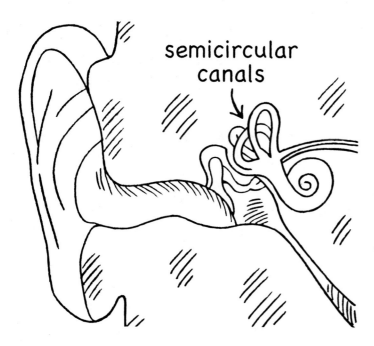

semicircular canals

Maggie still felt dizzy after stopping twirling because of a liquid. The liquid was in part of Maggie's ears. There are three parts to our ears. The three parts are the outer, middle, and inner parts. The inner ear has two parts. The two parts of the inner ear are the cochlea and semicircular canals. The three semicircular canals are half-circle-shaped tubes. The tubes contain liquid.

Even the slightest, or smallest, movement will cause the liquid in the semicircular canals to move. When the liquid moves, nerve cells are triggered. Once triggered, the nerve-cell endings send signals to the brain. The signals allow the brain to control one's sense of balance. Maggie stopped twirling, but her brain continued to get signals that she was spinning. This was because after all her rapid twirling, it took a while for the liquid in Maggie's ears to stop moving.

All the time that the liquid was still moving, nerve cells were still being triggered. The brain continued to get signals that made it think Maggie was still twirling. It was not until the liquid had stopped and the brain had stopped getting signals that Maggie stopped feeling dizzy.

To prevent feelings of dizziness, Maggie learned to stare at a spot straight ahead of her as she turned her body. As her body kept on turning, Maggie learned how to turn her head to look again at the same spot. By staring at the same spot, Maggie was able to maintain her sense of balance and prevent feelings of dizziness. This was because staring at the same spot kept the liquid in her ears from moving out of control.

Stopping Dizziness

After reading the story, answer the questions.
Fill in the circle next to the correct answer.

1. The semicircular canals are in what part of our ears?

   ⓐ inner
   ⓑ outer
   ⓒ liquid
   ⓓ middle

2. What item most likely has a semicircular shape?

   ⓐ a door
   ⓑ a trail
   ⓒ a carpet
   ⓓ a rainbow

3. This story is mainly about

   ⓐ ice skating.
   ⓑ what causes dizziness.
   ⓒ what signals our brains.
   ⓓ how nerves are triggered.

4. Why did staring at one spot help prevent Maggie from feeling dizzy?

   ⓐ it made it so Maggie could twirl rapidly
   ⓑ it triggered the nerve cells to signal her brain
   ⓒ it helped control the movement of liquid in her ears
   ⓓ it stopped Maggie from maintaining her sense of balance

5. Think about how the word *triggered* relates to *started*. What two words relate in the same way?

   triggered : started

   ⓐ felt : spun
   ⓑ moved : learned
   ⓒ continued : ended
   ⓓ prevented : stopped

The Rabbit Battle

These are new words to practice.

Say each word 10 times.

* native

* released

* descendent

* predator

* sparse

* vegetation

* imported

* immune

**Before or after reading the story, write one sentence
that contains at least one new word.**

_____

_____

_____

_____

The Rabbit Battle

In the early 1900s, a fence was built. It was over 2,000 miles (3,200 km) long! Who built the fence? Why was it built? The Australian government built the fence. It was hoped that it would stop rabbits from spreading into southwestern Australia. Rabbits are not native to Australia. Thomas Austin released, or set free, 24 rabbits in 1859. Austin released his rabbits so that he could hunt them.

The rabbit population got out of control. In just 18 months, a single pair of rabbits can have up to 184 descendents! A descendent is like a child or a baby. It is a person or thing that comes from a certain source. Rabbits had few natural enemies in Australia's native wildlife. There were few predators to keep the population down. A predator is one that lives by killing or eating other animals.

There were more than one billion rabbits in Australia by 1900. The rabbits were doing great harm to the already sparse vegetation. When something is sparse, it is thinly spread. It is not thick or crowded. The rabbits were overeating. Plus, grazing rabbits were cutting off the plants closer to the ground than native grazers. This way of grazing was harming and killing native vegetation. Native animals could not find enough to eat. Farmers needed to protect their crops.

Did the fence work? No, it did not. The rabbits quickly broke through. The government tried importing foxes. When something is imported, it is brought in. Foxes are natural predators of rabbits. The foxes did not help. Why didn't the foxes help? The foxes preyed on native wildlife!

In the 1950s, the government infected the rabbits with a disease. The population went down 90 percent. Unfortunately, rabbits became immune to the disease. When one is immune, one is protected. One cannot get sick. Today, the rabbit battle goes on. The battle involves introducing new diseases. It involves using poison. It involves building fences. It involves destroying rabbit homes. If Thomas Austin were alive today, one wonders what he might think.

The Rabbit Battle

After reading the story, answer the questions.
Fill in the circle next to the correct answer.

1. This story is mainly about

    ⓐ rabbits and Australia.

    ⓑ building a fence to stop rabbits.

    ⓒ the man who released rabbits in Australia.

    ⓓ native Australian vegetation and wildlife.

2. How many rabbits did Thomas Austin release in Australia?

    ⓐ 24

    ⓑ 90

    ⓒ 184

    ⓓ 1859

3. Think about how the word *sparse* relates to *crowded*. What two words relate in the same way?

    | **sparse : crowded** |

    ⓐ released : freed

    ⓑ native : imported

    ⓒ immune : protected

    ⓓ population : controlled

4. The rabbit battle today does not involve

    ⓐ using poison.

    ⓑ building fences.

    ⓒ destroying rabbit homes.

    ⓓ introducing new predators.

5. From the story, one can tell that

    ⓐ Thomas Austin is sorry for what he did.

    ⓑ Thomas Austin infected the rabbits with a disease.

    ⓒ Thomas Austin did not care about native vegetation.

    ⓓ Thomas Austin did not release his rabbits in the southwest.

Tornado Information

These are new words to practice.
Say each word 10 times.

✳ lodged	✳ declined
✳ tornado	✳ recent
✳ column	✳ decade
✳ funnel	✳ debris

Before or after reading the story, write one sentence that contains at least one new word.

_____

_____

_____

_____

Tornado Information

In 1950, a refrigerator was picked up near the town of Clyde, Texas. It was carried half a mile (.8 km) away. Then, it was lodged, or stuck firmly, high at the top of a telephone pole. What powerful force could be strong enough to lift a refrigerator, carry it away, and then lodge it high at the top of a telephone pole?

The powerful force is natural. It is a tornado. A tornado is a twisting column of air stretching between a thunderstorm and the ground. Often, the column looks like a funnel. A funnel is tube-shaped, with a wide cone at one end. Tornado winds can move at speeds of 300 miles (480 km) per hour or more. The winds are strong enough to lift heavy railroad cars right off the ground.

Tornados most often form out of thunderstorms during spring and summer. They have occurred all over the United States, but they are most common in an area nicknamed "Tornado Alley." Tornado Alley lies east of the Rocky Mountains. It extends through the central plains.

Why do so many tornados occur in Tornado Alley? First, cool, dry air flows down from Canada. The cool, dry air is funneled eastward by the Rocky Mountains. Second, warm, moist air flows northward from the Gulf of Mexico. Conditions are ripe for thunderstorms when the waves of cool, dry air and warm, moist air smash into each other over the central plains. The number of tornado-related deaths has declined, or lessened, in recent decades. A decade is a time period of 10 years.

Why have tornado-related deaths declined in recent decades? Early-warning systems have been developed. People know to stay away from windows and protect themselves from flying debris, or broken remains. They go to storm shelters or basements. If these are not available, they go to inside windowless rooms on the first floor. If they are outside or in a car, they go to a ditch or other low place away from the car. They use their arms to protect their head and neck from flying debris.

Tornado Information

**After reading the story, answer the questions.
Fill in the circle next to the correct answer.**

1. This story is mainly about
   (a) a powerful natural force.
   (b) where thunderstorms occur.
   (c) a refrigerator lodged on a pole.
   (d) being protected from flying debris.

2. An windowless room is most likely to be
   (a) a porch.
   (b) a closet.
   (c) a bedroom.
   (d) a kitchen.

3. A century is a time period of 100 years. How many decades are there in one century?
   (a) 1
   (b) 5
   (c) 10
   (d) 100

4. Which statement is true?
   (a) All tornadoes occur in Tornado Alley.
   (b) Tornado Alley is west of the Rocky Mountains.
   (c) Tornadoes in Tornado alley have recently declined.
   (d) Cool, dry air from Canada flows into Tornado Alley.

5. Think about how the word *declined* relates to *lessened*. What two words relate in the same way?

declined : lessened

   (a) used : smashed
   (b) lodged : stuck
   (c) cooled : warmed
   (d) protected : harmed

Answer Sheets

Student Name: _____

Title of Reading Passage: _____

_____

1. (a) (b) (c) (d)
2. (a) (b) (c) (d)
3. (a) (b) (c) (d)
4. (a) (b) (c) (d)
5. (a) (b) (c) (d)

Student Name: _____

Title of Reading Passage: _____

_____

1. (a) (b) (c) (d)
2. (a) (b) (c) (d)
3. (a) (b) (c) (d)
4. (a) (b) (c) (d)
5. (a) (b) (c) (d)

Bibliography

Allman, Toney. *Tapeworms.* KidHaven Press, Thomson Learning, Inc., 2004.

Angliss, Sarah. *Gold.* Benchmark Books, Marshall Cavendish Corporation, 2000.

Arreola, Daniel D., and Marci Smith Deal and James F. Petersen and Rickie Sanders. *World Geography.* McDougal Littell, Inc., 2003.

Associated Press. "Tallest Man's Long Arms Save Dolphins from Doom." *Journal and Courier.* 15 December, 2006: A2.

Ayer, Eleanor. *Lewis Latimer: Creating Bright Ideas.* Steck-Vaughn Company, 1997.

Brummitt, Chris. "No End in Sight for Indonesia's Mud Volcano." *Journal and Courier.* 29 September, 2006: A6.

Casselman, Anne. "Charting the Whale Shark Universe." *Discover.* July 2006: 13.

Cohen, Brad, and Lisa Wysocky. *Front of the Class: How Tourette Syndrome Made Me the Teacher I Never Had.* VanderWyk & Burnham, 2005.

Colapinto, John. "Bloodsuckers." *The New Yorker.* 25 July, 2005: 72-81.

Cooper, Jason. *Tarantulas.* Rourke Publishing LLC, 2006.

Daily, Robert. *The Sun.* Franklin Watts, 1994.

Day, Trevor. *The Random House Book of 1001 Questions and Answers about the Human Body.* Random House, Inc., 1994.

Editors, Secrets of the Universe. "Pluto and Charon." *Secrets of the Universe, The Solar System, Card 20.* International Masters Publishers AB.

———. "Space Suits." *Secrets of the Universe, Space Technology, Card 7.* International Masters Publishers AB.

———. "Yuri Gagarin." *Secrets of the Universe, Space Pioneers, Card 2.* International Masters Publishers AB.

Farris, Katherine, Editor. *You Asked? Over 300 Great Questions and Astounding Answers.* Owl Books, 1996.

Grace, Catherine O'Neill. *Forces of Nature: The Awesome Power of Volcanoes, Earthquakes, and Tornadoes.* National Geographic Society, 2004.

Grandin, Karl, Editor. *Les Prix Nobel. The Nobel Prizes 2005.* Nobel Foundation, 2006.

Kamler, Kenneth, M.D. *Surviving the Extremes.* St. Martin's Press, 2004.

Kent, Jacqueline C. *Women in Medicine.* The Oliver Press, Inc., 1998.

Kleeman, Elise. "Space Junk." *Discover.* November 2006: 20.

Krulwich, Robert. "Dig a Hole to China? Try a Sandwich Instead." *NPR Weekend Edition.* 17 June, 2006.

Bibliography *(cont.)*

Lampton, Christopher. *Endangered Species.* Franklin Watts, 1988.

Lilly, Melinda. *Salt.* Rourke Publishing, LLC, 2002.

Marriott, Edward. *Plague: A Story of Science, Rivalry, and the Scourge That Won't Go Away.*
Metropolitan Books, Henry Holt and Company, LLC, 2002.

Mattern, Joanne. *Joseph E. Murray and the Story of the First Human Kidney Transplant.*
    Mitchell Lane Publishers, 2003.

McCutcheon, Marc. *The Kid Who Named Pluto and the Stories of Other Extraordinary Young
    People in Science.* Chronicle Books, LLC., 2004.

Middleton, Nick. *Extremes: Surviving the World's Harshest Environments.* Thomas Dunne
    Books, St. Martin's Press, 2003.

Nielsen, Nancy J. *Carnivorous Plants.* Franklin Watts, 1992.

"Passenger Pigeon." *The New Encyclopedia Britannica*, volume 9, page 185. Encyclopedia
    Britannica, Inc., 1990.

Royston, Angela. *Why Do I Get A Toothache?: And Other Questions About Nerves.*
Heinemann Library, Reed Education & Professional Publishing, 2003.

Ruvinsky, Jessica. "World's Smallest GPS System." *Discover.* October 2006: 15.

Silverstein, Alvin, and Virginia Silverstein and Laura Silverstein Nunn. *Symbiosis.* Twenty-
First Century Books, The Millbrook Press, Inc., 1998.

Simon, Seymour. *Guts: Our Digestive System.* HarperCollins Publishers, 2005.

———. *The Heart.* William Morrow and Company, Inc., 1996.

Sparrow, Giles. *Iron.* Benchmark Books, Marshall Cavendish Corporation, 1999.

Stone, Alex. "Fuzzy Math: The Monty Hall Scenario." *Discover.* July 2006: 15.

———. "Pluto Demoted." *Discover.* January 2007: 31.

Tocci, Salvatore. *The Periodic Table.* Children's Press, Scholastic Inc., 2004.

Twist, Clint. *Cockroaches.* Gareth Stevens Publishing, 2006.

Welsbacher, Anne. *Whale Sharks.* Capstone Press, 1995.

Wexo, John Bonnett. *Zoobooks: Giraffes.* Wildlife Education Ltd., 1991.

Wilkes, Angela. *Dangerous Creatures.* Kingfisher Publications, 2003.

Wood, Richard and Sara. *Dian Fossey.* Heinemann Library, Reed Educational & Professional
    Publishing, 2001.

Answer Key

A Tarantula and Duct Tape
1. A   4. D
2. C   5. A
3. C

Space Junk
1. A   4. B
2. A   5. C
3. D

Gorilla Lady
1. D   4. B
2. C   5. B
3. C

Why We Get Goose Bumps
1. C   4. D
2. A   5. B
3. A

Strange Partners
1. A   4. D
2. D   5. B
3. C

A Brilliant Element
1. C   4. A
2. C   5. D
3. B

Digging a Hole to China
1. A   4. C
2. B   5. D
3. A

A Picture to Remember
1. D   4. C
2. B   5. D
3. B

A Whale of a Fish
1. A   4. C
2. D   5. D
3. B

Saving Richard Herrick
1. C   4. D
2. B   5. B
3. C

Dressing for Survival
1. A   4. D
2. A   5. D
3. C

Two to Trigger
1. B   4. D
2. A   5. A
3. B

An Expedition for Bloodsuckers
1. D   4. C
2. B   5. A
3. B

All About Feet
1. A   4. D
2. D   5. B
3. C

Surviving Without a Head
1. D   4. C
2. C   5. B
3. D

The Substance Answer
1. D   4. D
2. B   5. A
3. B

The "She" in the Tongue Twister
1. C   4. D
2. B   5. A
3. C

Two Strange Eruptions
1. D   4. A
2. A   5. C
3. D

A Parasite's Greatest Enemy
1. D   4. B
2. D   5. A
3. A

What Color Was the Bear?
1. B   4. D
2. A   5. C
3. B

A Different Walk
1. B   4. A
2. A   5. C
3. C

A Spy or an Alien?
1. A   4. B
2. B   5. D
3. C

Why Pig Bristles Were Glued to Ants
1. D   4. C
2. C   5. D
3. B

Getting Sick on Purpose
1. B   4. D
2. D   5. C
3. C

Where Days Are Different Lengths
1. A   4. D
2. A   5. B
3. B

All About Smelling
1. B   4. C
2. A   5. C
3. A

Name that Mammal!
1. D   4. C
2. D   5. B
3. B

The Eiffel Tower, Meteorites, and Our Diet
1. C   4. B
2. A   5. A
3. C

Out-of-Control Twitching
1. C   4. B
2. D   5. D
3. A

Pus — A Sign of Battle
1. C   4. C
2. B   5. D
3. D

An Inventor Who Was Paid Less
1. B   4. A
2. C   5. D
3. C

A Huge Area in a Small Space
1. D   4. B
2. C   5. D
3. B

The Changing Planet Number
1. A   4. D
2. B   5. A
3. C

Why a Termite Eats Its Skin
1. B   4. C
2. D   5. B
3. A

Making Bread Taste Sweet
1. D   4. C
2. B   5. B
3. D

Donya's Guides
1. B   4. A
2. C   5. A
3. D

The Last Pigeon
1. D   4. A
2. B   5. A
3. B

A Doctor Who Listened with Fingertips
1. B   4. D
2. C   5. C
3. B

The Wrong Door
1. C   4. B
2. A   5. A
3. B

The Tall Man Solution
1. D   4. C
2. C   5. A
3. B

The Cent with a Scent
1. D   4. C
2. B   5. A
3. C

Stopping Dizziness
1. A   4. C
2. D   5. D
3. B

The Rabbit Battle
1. A   4. D
2. A   5. D
3. B

Tornado Information
1. A   4. D
2. B   5. B
3. C